Guest-Based Marketing

Guest-Based Marketing

How to Increase Restaurant Sales Without Breaking Your Budget

Bill Marvin

The Restaurant Doctor™

JOHN WILEY & SONS, INC.

New York • Chichester • Weinheim • Brisbane • Singapore • Toronto

Library of Congress Cataloging-in-Publication Data

Marvin, Bill.
    Guest-based marketing : how to increase restaurant sales without breaking your budget / Bill Marvin.
        p.   cm.
    Includes index.
    ISBN 0-471-15394-X (cloth : alk. paper)
    1. Restaurants—Marketing.   2. Food service management.
    TX911.3.M3M38   1997
    647.95'068'8—dc20   96-51707

*To the memory of my father, Ed Marvin, who truly understood
that success in all activities, professional and personal,
is about taking care of people*

Contents

Give Guests Something Good to Talk About   61

Provide Incentives to Return   117

Opening Observations

Preface

Customers for life. The idea is so simple and so elusive. All it means is that you operate in such a way that once guests are exposed to your restaurant, they will never be satisfied with any of your competitors. It means that your serious sales-building work happens on the floor with the guests, not in the office with the marketing plan and advertising schedule.

I maintain that the focus of foodservice management should not be to make a profit but to make sure that the guests are happy. I also concede that management skill is ultimately measured by the consistent profitability of the operation, but focusing on the bottom line alone will not assure success.

If you take care of your guests, your sales will tend to take care of themselves. If the sales volume is there, the odds are that your costs will be in line.

Evolution of an Idea

If you accept that profitability is what enables you to continue to play the game, my books represent a logical progression toward helping operators do a better job of pleasing guests at a profit.

My book *Restaurant Basics* deals with the small irritations that can accumulate and cause guests to become disenchanted. It is the only book on customer service written entirely from the guests' point of view and effectively defines the actions that diners lump into the category of "bad attitude."

The Foolproof Foodservice Selection System is about how to get the right people . . . the first time. You cannot make quality products with substandard ingredients and your staff is the raw ingredient in your service recipe.

Then came *From Turnover to Teamwork*, which describes how you can keep those good people once you have found them. More specifically, it is about how you can run your organization in such a way that people want to hang out with you! The environment that causes your staff to stay is the same environment that causes your guests to want to return more often.

The groundwork having been laid, now comes *Guest-Based Marketing* which discusses how to build volume from your existing customer base. It is an examination of the factors that make yours the restaurant of choice for diners who increasingly have more options to choose from. It provides practical, tested ideas that can help you create the sort of experience that will draw guests back again and again . . . and at little or no cost.

Groundwork is important. You cannot entice guests back to a restaurant where they were treated impersonally or unprofessionally. This uncaring attitude is more likely to be displayed by staff members who were hired haphazardly into a restaurant with a poor work climate and low operating standards.

Now that all the pieces are in place, we are ready to examine the principles that will cause diners to be delighted with the restaurant, vocal in their support, and loyal in their patronage.

Restaurant Reality

Every restaurateur I know is engaged in the exercise of increasing (or trying to increase) sales. There seems to be some sort of preoccupation with the notion that bigger is better or that if we do not exceed last year's sales we are somehow falling behind. Both of these points are debatable, but the obsession with maintaining growth is undeniably a stress factor for many operators.

The increasing number of competitors in the market only complicates the process and adds to the frustration. In addition to the normal increase in independent operations, many chains are now entering second- and third-tier markets as their primary markets reach saturation.

Multi-Unit Operators

Chains are serious competitors who bring some real clout to the market. Their sheer size evokes a fear response in many independent operators. They typically have a clearer sense of identity in the market and may enjoy a positive reputation before they even open.

Typically multi-unit operators can bring more professional expertise to the market if for no other reason than that they have more money and can buy what they need. In many markets, chains are a breath of freshness. They are certainly serious about what they do and have a depth of capital that makes them hard to beat.

But chains also have vulnerabilities. They are not local and the need for corporate control is often at odds with the need for market responsiveness at the unit level. Chain restaurants are often impersonal and can leave guests with a feeling of being processed rather than being served. Their "cookie counter" consistency has pros and cons but often can be a disadvantage.

Chains are necessarily slower to react and less flexible in dealing with unique problem-solving than their independent counterparts. Their focus is often more on costs and percentages than it is on making the guest happy. Their managers typically have less latitude to be experimental.

Independent Operators

Independents are at a disadvantage for many of the reasons noted above, but they also have some advantages that a chain cannot match. The typical independent has a local identity. The operation was started by someone from the area to serve people in the area. Since hospitality is a business based on personal connection, the local tie can be a strong plus. Interestingly, independents may be seen as more personal and friendly because of their imperfections.

Many locally owned restaurants literally grew up with the owners and reflect the learning curve in uniquely quirky ways. Independents have to answer to only themselves and the market, making them far more flexible than their chain competitors. A local restaurant will have a longer history or tradition than a recently arrived national or regional operation.

Without the need to support a corporate overhead and with sites that were developed when market prices for land and construction were lower, local operators often enjoy lower operating costs. This permits flexibility that is difficult for newcomers to match.

Independents can be more innovative than chains because they are more often operated by entrepreneurs. All successful chain concepts grew from an entrepreneurial dream that worked! Chain executives are quick to admit that they are better at growing an idea than they are at conceiving the idea in the first place.

Finally, the local operator has an established staff, often with workers who have served guests for generations. There is a legacy there that no chain will be able to match.

My point in bringing all this up is that competition is a fact of life. If you are successful, someone will move in beside you to try to get a piece of your business. But no matter where the competition comes from, the savvy operator will play off of his or her strongest market advantages to stay ahead. Too often local restaurateurs try to compete head-on with the newcomers—a stressful tactic at best.

Don't Compete—EXCEL!

Nearly every market I visit is experiencing a major influx of new restaurants, and it doesn't matter if they are chain operations with deep pockets and smooth formats or independents trying to carve out a niche or pursue a dream. In either case, operators are spending more and more time worrying about the market, looking over their shoulders, counting cars, and trying to outguess the new guys.

When they ask me what they should do, I tell them to stop trying to compete! Competing can be dangerous to your professional survival! Let me explain: Have you ever been driving down the road and had a police car behind you? I don't know about you but when that happens to me, I suddenly become fixated on the speedometer and fascinated by the rear view mirror. In this condition, I have a lot less time to pay attention to where I am going! The closer an eye I keep on the cop, the higher my anxiety level rises. I am definitely not as good a driver when I am watching the car behind me.

The same thing applies in the business world. When you are watching the competition, it drains vital energy away from your primary focus, which should be on making sure you take excellent care of your guests and run the very best restaurant you can. An obsession with your competitors can interfere with giving your guests a memorable experience! Wake up!

Be competitive . . . but don't compete. Monetary success and personal joy will come when your sole concern—your driving passion—is only how you can excel!

The Best Defense

The best competitive strategy is to never let your guests get to the competition. Every time a guest eats with you is one less shot anyone else has to impress them and win their patronage. So not only do you get the sales but your competitors do not have a chance to make an impression and win them over.

People are creatures of habit and once the habit is formed, they are not likely to break it . . . unless you give them a reason to do so. But they only come back because they want to! Therefore the safest way to build sales is to foster repeat business and to be sure that your guests know all the wonderful things you do for them so that they will be sure to think of you on those rare occasions when they dine elsewhere.

Shrinking Market Area

Building volume from existing guests makes sense geographically. As competition increases, as more and more restaurants enter the market, the distance people are willing to drive to a restaurant is steadily declining.

Mike Hurst of 15th Street Fisheries in Fort Lauderdale, Florida, estimates that ten years ago, his guests traveled 15–20 miles for dinner. Today, he says, the majority of his diners live within 2½ miles of his restaurant and the radius is slowly tightening. People may drive past two or three other restaurants to get to you but, unless you are a serious destination restaurant, they are not likely to drive past 20 or 30.

Guest-Based Marketing

So your most realistic option to build sales has to come from guests who are already within the acceptable travel distance . . . and your dining room is full of them! The trick now is to be able to get them back again and again, and that is the basis of what we are calling GBM, or Guest-Based Marketing.

You will find the following pages full of hints on how to build volume from your existing customer base without losing your shirt in the process. But a word of caution before we get started: You will do better to understand the reasoning behind the ideas offered than to simply adopt the ideas. The notions I present are not extensively documented for precisely that reason. Too much detail might make this look like a how-to book when it is really a why-to book. Not every suggestion is appropriate for every restaurant (and adopting *all* of them is inappropriate for *any* restaurant)!

My goal is to increase your understanding of how to build volume from your existing customer base, not necessarily to put more toys in your toy box. If you understand what I am pointing to and the principles that make it work, you will be able to identify and implement your own unique programs and never run out of ideas.

I encourage you to share your stories, both good and bad, and to contact me with any comments, suggestions, or questions. My address and phone are included at the end of the book for just that purpose. Good luck and have fun!

Bill Marvin, The Restaurant Doctor™
Gig Harbor, Washington
February 1997

Guest-Based Marketing

Build Loyalty, Not the Check Average

1

Selling Techniques Can Be Dangerous

I realize that I may be trifling with a religious tenet of modern restaurant management here, but we are squarely in the age of service and I must point out an unpopular truth—the use of suggestive selling techniques can be dangerous to your professional survival! (Take a minute to catch your breath and still your pounding heart!)

I know you do not want to hear it. I know you want to believe that the salvation of your restaurant will be assured if only your staff would get with the suggestive selling program and pull up those check averages.

Well, I hate to be the bearer of bad news, but the truth is that the emperor does not have any clothes on . . . and perhaps never did.

This obituary might be easier to accept if you did not have so much time, energy, money, and professional ego invested in pushing the idea of suggestive selling to your staff. But the clues have been there all along.

See if any of the following strike a familiar cord:

- You have invested at least 38,000 man-hours lecturing your staff about the importance of increasing the check average.
- You have put untold dollars into books, tapes, and posters about suggestive selling.
- You have made detailed financial calculations showing how much your service staff can increase their tips if they would only sell appetizers to one party in four.
- You have changed everybody's job title from server to salesperson.
- You have kept track of check averages and rewarded those with the highest averages or greatest increases.

- You have given the best stations or the choicest schedules to the people with the highest check averages.
- You have run sales contests with fabulous prizes—a few people do well and everyone else ignores you.
- You have fired (or threatened to fire) people because their check average was too low.
- You have lamented to your staff that sales were declining and hinted that if the check averages did not improve . . .

You have put out all this effort and chances are that 95% of your service staff are still digging in their heels and fighting you about suggestive selling!

What's wrong with this picture? It's time to wake up! The members of your service staff are not dummies. If they thought suggestive selling was in their own best interests, they would already be doing it. But they are savvy business people. They see the danger and they are not going to cut their own throats.

So what do they see that you may have missed? Perhaps they truly understand that their money comes from serving people, not from serving food.

2

Job One

Foodservice is a service business and that means that Job One has to be making sure our guests are happy.

As an operator, I always knew that keeping the guest happy was one of the things I wanted to do, but it was on the list with repairing the ice machine, working out the new menu, and the dozens of other things I had to handle! It has only been in the last few years that I have come to realize at a very gut level that the principal job an operator should focus on is making sure the guests are happy.

If they're not, you are in big trouble! If the people leaving your restaurant are not thrilled by what happened inside your walls, who cares what your check average is?

To put it into perspective, ponder this: If everyone who had ever eaten in your restaurant was so pleased that they could not wait to come back and could not wait to tell their friends about you, what kind of sales volume would you be doing?

Certainly more than you are doing now. I will suggest that you really have no idea what sort of volume you are capable of doing. But it all has to start with making your guests happy.

3

The Problem with Selling Techniques

Every foodservice operator wants to build sales. If traffic levels are relatively flat, the approach most people take to building sales is to try to increase the per person expenditure (average check) by implementing an aggressive program using suggestive selling techniques.

I fully acknowledge that, done with sincerity and skill, suggestive selling can enhance the dining experience for some guests. It can even raise the check average and increase short-term sales. Unfortunately, building sales by pumping the check can easily backfire.

How Does the Guest Feel?

Done poorly (and most servers do it poorly because they do not believe in it), suggestive selling can easily come across to your guests as insincere, shallow, and manipulative.

A number of operators have even confessed to me that they can tell when a server in a competitor's restaurant has just "read the selling book" or "had the selling lecture" because they feel like the sales machine has been unleashed on them. The techniques are obvious and impersonal. It is interesting that operators will notice it in a competitor's operation but miss the same thing when it is happening under their own roof!

The sad truth is that, for most patrons, suggestive selling as commonly practiced does not leave them with a comfortable feeling or make them anxious to volunteer for more. A number of diners have shared that they find the practice insulting. In discussing his reactions to server suggestions, one man told me, "I am over 50 years old. I know that they have Chivas Regal at the bar. If that was what I wanted, I would have asked for it!"

If you have a deal to offer, that is a slightly different situation. But to make the suggestion for the sole purpose of increasing the amount of money a guest spends does not serve the guest and, in the end, does not serve the operator.

Who Is Important Here?

That may be the heart of the problem. Selling techniques emphasize the needs of the operator rather than the needs of the guests. If you accept that Job One is making the guests happy, then success requires that your primary emphasis be on identifying what the guests want and making sure they are getting it consistently.

A successful operation must focus all its energy on the guest. Any time the focus shifts away from the guest, you risk the patrons feeling diminished, less well-served, and less anxious to return.

An attendee in one of my seminars offered the observation that building sales by pushing the check might be a way for operators to avoid taking responsibility for the sales volume. It is not difficult to imagine a tired restaurateur thinking, "If only those lazy waitresses would get off their butts and bring the check average up, we would be in great shape."

A more subtle danger is that when you or your staff fixate on how much money people are spending, it can be a distraction that gets in the way of establishing a good rapport with your guests. You might get the big sale tonight and lose the guests' future patronage. If that should happen, then pushing the check average was not a smart strategy for maximizing long-term income.

4

Raising Revenues

L et's say your typical guest comes in twice a month and your average check per person is $10. Let's also say that you would like a 50% sales increase (who wouldn't?)! What are your options?

Option 1: Increase the Check Average

Well, you could try to increase your average check to $15 and hope that people would still come in as often as they did before. You might be able to pull this off, but I would not want to bet on it. Most operators I have talked with feel that their guests have a certain amount of money they are comfortable spending in any given situation. The chances are that creating pressure to increase the per person expenditure could result in lowered overall guest counts. Raising the average check is not likely to work.

Option 2: Invest in Promotion

You could invest heavily in promotion, but that can also be very expensive. Every cost you add raises the sales required to net out a 50% increase. Besides, the odds of coming up with a campaign that would produce a consistent 50% sales increase are also pretty slim. Promotion is usually not the answer.

Option 3: Increase Frequency

What are the odds that you could treat your guests in such a way that instead of coming in twice a month, they would come in three times a month? Pretty good, I'll bet. Just one more visit a month would provide that 50% sales increase . . . without any increase in average check and without any increased pressure on the guests or your service staff! If you can give your guests such a good experience that they come to you instead of patronizing your competition, you cannot help but increase your volume.

Do you see how it works? A 50% sales increase seems impossible, but getting guests to come back one more time a month seems pretty reasonable. And it is. After all, your guests are eating *somewhere*, why shouldn't it be with you? Even if guests come in twice a *week*, one more visit a month still translates into a 12½% sales increase, again without any pressure to increase the average check.

The safest way to achieve sales growth is to have your guests return more often. In this mode, your goal is to delight your guests, win their trust, and earn their loyalty rather than simply trying to increase the average per person sale.

Don't get me wrong—if a guest wants to spend more money, I have absolutely no problem in taking it with gratitude and a smile! But it is about time we stopped having such a fixation on how much our guests spend on each visit and started putting our energies toward increasing the number of times they visit!

Now the two are not necessarily incompatible—it is possible to build both repeat patronage *and* the check average. However, I place the focus on the human side of the equation because foodservice is a business based on personal relationships.

I do not believe that success in building the average per person sale will guarantee guest loyalty or repeat patronage, nor will it necessarily sustain long-term sales growth. On the other hand, I firmly believe that success in building guest loyalty and repeat patronage will always increase total revenue and sustain it over the long term.

5

Understanding Service

Our primary job in the foodservice industry is to give our guests a wonderful experience. If our guests do not enjoy themselves, nothing else really matters.

Think about that for a minute. Many operators spend an inordinate amount of time concerned with hiring, cost controls, financial decisions, and marketing issues. They spend five times the effort trying to reduce food cost half a point than they do finding ways to increase sales and have guests return more frequently.

To paraphrase service guru Peter Glen, good service is just finding out what people want, determining how they want it . . . and giving it to them just that way.

A Shining Example

Good service comes from satisfying your guests. Legendary service comes from delighting your guests by totally exceeding their expectations. Here is an example:

> It was a warm evening in early June—the night of the senior prom. Two lovely young women sat in a Spokane, Washington, restaurant waiting for their dates to arrive. The wait stretched on and eventually it became obvious that the dates were not coming. Just another teenage tragedy, right?

In most cases, probably so. But Beth Sayers, dinner manager at Clinkerdagger's Restaurant, was touched by their plight. She asked the girls if they would mind being escorted to the prom by two of her waiters she recruited to be Prince Charmings.

She obtained the requisite approvals from the girls' parents. She even got the approval of one waiter's wife, who was thrilled that her

Australian-born husband would have a chance to see a slice of typical Americana! The restaurant not only supplied the dates, but paid for the hors d'oeuvres the girls had eaten while they waited. Sayers even gave the waiters money to pay for pictures and other expenses at the prom.

Commenting to the local media, Sayers said, "Sure it was a nice thing, but what the girls did was far more coura-

---

GUEST SERVICE CHECKLIST

To assess your level of guest service, answer these questions honestly. Avoid wishful thinking. Mark "Y" if the results are always achieved, "N" if the results are not regularly obtained and "?" if the outcome varies. For a more accurate picture, have all your staff members complete the checklist anonymously. It might be revealing to ask some of your regular guests for their opinions as well.

Y N ?

☐☐☐ The company has a written philosophy of guest gratification that is integral to all orientation/training activities.

☐☐☐ All company procedures and decisions are based on what is best for the guest.

☐☐☐ Management has developed an effective, well-conceived strategy for guest service that is consistently delivered.

☐☐☐ Staff members consistently focus on delighting the guests.

☐☐☐ Top management consistently demonstrates their commitment to guest gratification in words <u>and</u> actions.

☐☐☐ Managers actively determine what their guests want and how the organization can exceed guest expectations.

☐☐☐ Staff members consistently behave in a friendly and courteous manner toward guests.

☐☐☐ Staff members consistently reinforce the guests' feelings of self-worth.

☐☐☐ Staff members consistently and effectively convey their genuine interest in helping the guests.

☐☐☐ Staff members consistently provide proper meal pacing.

☐☐☐ Staff members consistently observe teamwork practices which focus on the needs of the guests.

☐☐☐ Staff members have a feeling of being a professional and of being important to the organization and the guests.

☐☐☐ Staff members consistently anticipate problems rather than waiting until the guests complain.

☐☐☐ Staff members know how their work should be done and consistently meet job-related standards.

☐☐☐ Staff members provide knowledgeable answers to all guest questions.

☐☐☐ Staff members consistently wear the appropriate uniform which is kept neat and clean.

☐☐☐ Staff members consistently contact their supervisor about potential conflict situations involving guests.

☐☐☐ Staff members consistently treat guests the way the guests want to be treated.

☐☐☐ Staff members consistently provide an equal level of service to <u>all</u> guests.

☐☐☐ Staff members consistently give their undivided attention when interacting with guests.

☐☐☐ Staff members consistently demonstrate the politeness and respect due all persons.

☐☐☐ Staff members consistently observe the proper procedures for resolving guests' complaints.

☐☐☐ Staff members never make excuses and promptly resolve complaints in favor of the guest.

☐☐☐ Staff members consistently maintain "smiling eye contact" when speaking with guests.

☐☐☐ Staff members consistently go out of their way to accommodate special guest needs.

☐☐☐ Staff members consistently acknowledge guests' arrival with a smile and eye contact within 30 seconds.

☐☐☐ Staff members consistently observe proper telephone etiquette.

☐☐☐ Guests are consistently thanked for their patronage as they arrive and again as they leave.

☐☐☐ Staff members consistently address regular guests by name.

☐☐☐ Staff members consistently pay attention to details regarding all work that they do.

Source: Adapted from "Food Service Management by Checklist" by Brother Herman E. Zaccarelli with permission of John Wiley & Sons, ©1991

Figure 5-1

geous. We had the easy part. In the face of embarrassment and humiliation, these girls went to their prom."

Now THAT is legendary service. Its focus is on what it takes to make the guest happy and does not limit itself to the daily mechanics of running a restaurant.

How Is Your Service?

This might be a good time for a little self-evaluation. Figure 5-1 sets forth a number of elements of guest service that are worth a look. For this exercise to be meaningful, it is important that you approach it honestly. Wishful thinking as a way to improve your "score" will only serve to keep opportunities for improvement hidden from you. You can count on your guests to notice what you don't.

Remember that this is a business based on personal connection and happy guests. The secret of GBM is building repeat patronage . . .

. . . and guests only come back because they *want to!*

6

Sunset Grill: A Case Study

My current favorite-restaurant-on-the-planet is Sunset Grill in Nashville, Tennessee. The proprietor, Randy Rayburn, is a savvy restaurateur who keeps close tabs on his operation. He tracks the number of people who walk in the door every day and he records how many patrons specifically request to be seated at each server's station . . .

. . . *but Randy has never calculated his check average!*

It's true. When you go to Sunset Grill, neither Randy or anyone on his service staff is concerned about how much money you spend—they just want to be sure you have a wonderful time and come back soon! So whether you spend $10 or $100 (and you can easily do either!) you get the same careful attention—a classic case of building loyalty and not the check average.

How well is it working? Nashville probably has 50% more restaurant seats than it did a few years ago. Over that same period, Randy reports that sales at Sunset Grill are up over 100% in 3 years! (Admittedly, he has put two additions on the restaurant in that time, but he would not have invested in the extra space if he did not need it!) Has competition in your market increased that much? Are your sales up that much?

One other small point: Nashville has an unemployment rate of less than 2½%. It is not at all unusual for a restaurant to advertise for help and receive three applications in three weeks. In this same market, Randy has a waiting list of qualified people who want to come to work with him!

There may be an unexpected downside in all this success, however. Randy recently needed to hire another manager and solicited his service staff for applicants. He came up empty. None of his servers could afford the cut in pay!

Maybe Randy is on to something.

Focus on Guest Delight

7

Satisfaction Stinks

When it comes to service, everyone talks about the importance of making sure your guests are satisfied. Satisfaction is certainly better than dissatisfaction, but in today's competitive market, satisfaction will not be enough to keep you growing and prospering over the long term.

As the foodservice pie gets sliced into more and more pieces, it is important to go beyond mere satisfaction and become memorable in the eyes of your guests. To be memorable, you must not only *meet* your guests' expectations, you must *exceed* them.

In other words, you must make sure your guests are *delighted!*

Delight Differs from Satisfaction

Diner delight is more important than good service because it has a different focus. As we already mentioned, the problem with talking to your staff about good service is that it is too easy to define service from the perspective of the person providing it.

> Manager: "Did you give them good service?"
>
> Server: "Yes, I did!"
>
> Manager: "Well then, why haven't they been back?"

What makes delight so powerful is that it cannot be defined from the server's point of view. To see if the guest is delighted, you must look at the dining experience from the guest's perspective—the only point of view that really matters!

Focusing on delight will force you to see everything that happens in the restaurant through your guests' eyes, and that will keep you more in touch with their dining experience.

An important point to understand: *hospitality is based on personal connection, not on technical execution.*

Service Differs from Hospitality

Service is about technical execution. It is about timing. It is about things like serving from the left, clearing from the right, and not dribbling wine on the tablecloth. The technical execution is important but it is not likely to delight guests except perhaps in comparison to more inept competitors.

Hospitality, on the other hand, is about personal connection. It is about *me* taking care of *you* . . . because it is *YOU* . . . not because you are one of 75 people who will go through my station tonight.

In truth, you never serve 75 people anyway. You serve one person at a time in 75 different scenarios. The more personal that interaction is and the more it exceeds the diner's expectations, the more delighted the guest will be.

The Domino Effect

The value of a happy guest is that a patron who has an enjoyable experience will tell five others about it, starting a progression that can make you very successful indeed.

Now if that guest is *delighted*—if he has received more than he expected from people who established personal connection and caring—he is more likely to tell other people. His enthusiasm will be contagious and you are more likely to get trial from the people he tells.

So delight is the result of exceeding guests' expectations with personal connection and caring acts. Expectations are outlined in Chapters 8-10. Chapters 11-20 outline some of the delightful touches I have seen in restaurants over the past several years. The personal quality most responsible for establishing human connection is presence, discussed in Chapter 57.

8

Expectations

It may help to think of the quality of your guests' dining experience as a game. Because people want to have a good time in restaurants, you start this game with a perfect score, say 100 points. As guests approach the restaurant and progress through their meal, you gain or lose points.

It is the details that can raise or lower your score. There are literally thousands of things for which you will *lose* points when they happen but you won't necessarily *gain* points if they don't. It is not necessarily fair, but it is the way human nature works. For a thousand or so of them, see my book *Restaurant Basics*.

But our focus here is on delight, and if you want to delight your guests, you need to look for those unexpected touches for which you can *gain* points and improve your score.

State of Mind

People's perceptions are a function of their state of mind—the mood they are in when we do what we do. The lower the mood gets, the more serious and threatening life appears to the guest. The more threatening something appears, the more points it costs you.

The same applies for pleasant surprises. When your guests receive something pleasant that they did not expect, it raises their mood. The higher the mood gets, the more fun guests have. The food tastes better, the tips are higher, and the guests are more forgiving of minor service lapses.

So what do people expect?

9

Service Expectations

A merican Express' *Briefing* newsletter reported the results of a national study of restaurant service timing. The study was conducted by Performance Review, a New York hospitality consulting firm, and was based on 300 dinners at 40 restaurants with per person check averages of $25 or more. They calculated both average service timing and when customer complaints about service occur.

Figure 9-1 outlines the results of the study. Among other things, the study concluded that there is almost no such thing as service that is too fast, except delivering entrees too quickly, the #1 customer complaint about timing.

The study found that customer complaints seem to rise to significant levels 10 minutes after the average restaurant service time has passed. However, this 10-minute rule does not hold when guests are waiting for their first drink and for dessert. At the beginning and end of the meal, customers appear to be much less tolerant of delays.

Aside from helping to more clearly define guests' expectations relative to timing, the study suggests that a restaurant that can respond immediately to guests at the beginning and end of the meal

RESTAURANT AVERAGE	SERVICE CATEGORY	IDEAL RANGE
4 min, 12 sec	Initial Approach	1–2 min
3 min, 18 sec	Drink order to delivery	1–2 min
10 min, 3 sec	Appetizer order to delivery	5–10 min
21 min, 15 sec	Appetizer delivery to entree delivery	15–25 min
6 min, 35 sec	Dessert order to delivery	3–5 min
6 min, 45 sec	Check turnaround	1–2 min

Figure 9-1

and time the entree carefully could potentially accommodate an additional turn and still have happy patrons.

So one area where you can exceed expectations is in the area of service timing, although the points come primarily in comparison to competitors who do not do as good a job of managing the flow of service.

In addition to timing considerations, guests expect a basic level of competence on the part of the restaurant staff. They expect servers will know what items are on the menu, the ingredients in each, and how each dish is prepared. In restaurants with a wine list, guests expect servers to be able to answer basic questions about the wines on the list. They expect that the staff will follow appropriate sanitation procedures and they expect that their china, silverware, and glassware will be clean. They want servers to be neat and clean . . . and they expect people to care.

10

Product Expectations

Guests expect hot food to be hot and cold food to be cold . . . and very few people do it. If there is a cardinal culinary rule in the foodservice business, this is it. Still, restaurant cooks put hot food on cold plates or portion cold food onto plates hot from the dish machine every day.

If you can prepare food at the proper temperature, how do you get it to the guest that way? It is simple physics: If the plate is hotter than the food, it will raise the food's temperature. If it is colder, it will cool the food.

To serve cold food cold, you must chill the food to start with. Cold plates are simply a matter of refrigeration. Other than pre-portioned frozen desserts, do not store cold food plates in a freezer. Frozen plates are *too* cold and can freeze moist foods. You might want to bring a chilled fork when you serve a cold plate. A crisp, cool salad is simple, elegant, and memorable, particularly when you make guests aware of it.

Mike Hurst of Fort Lauderdale's 15th Street Fisheries tells his guests as he serves a cool bowl of chilled greens that 43°F is the perfect temperature for a salad. The statement creates a point of difference for his restaurant whenever his guests get a warm salad at another establishment. We discuss this idea further when we look at developing word of mouth.

Serving hot food hot becomes a little more involved. To be perceived as hot, food must reach the guest at close to 200°F. Food cooked to order is usually at least that hot. Check the temperature of items held on a steam table. Stir frequently to be sure they are up to temperature, preferably at least 180°F.

The second piece of this equation is the tricky part. Plates that are hot enough to keep food from cooling on the way to the table are too hot to hold in your bare hand. If you are serious about hot food, heat plates in the oven to around 250–300°F. Your staff must use a towel with plates that are this temperature, of course, but your guests will get hot food.

Here again, a little guest education will help you. As you place that hot food on the hot plate in front of the guest, you might say, "Watch out. Not only is that plate hot, but that food is hot, too. Not many restaurants do that any more!" The next time they visit a competitor and get an aggressively warm platter of food, who do you think will come to mind?

I also suggest removing your heat lamps. Your staff may think that heat lamps will keep waiting food hot. They will not. This false sense of security can delay getting hot food to your guests. Without heat lamps, there is an urgency when hot food is up.

11

Delightful Practices

Presence (see Chapter 57) is the human dimension of delight, but there is also an action side. Delight results from actually *doing* something to demonstrate your degree of caring.

In the following chapters, I outline some practices I have observed that were unexpected and delightful for the diners involved. This is not an exhaustive list—there are always new and exciting touches that arise spontaneously in the moment when your head is clear and you are focused on delight.

Not every item mentioned is appropriate for every restaurant or under every circumstance—these are just some examples to get you thinking. Readers of *Restaurant Basics* may recognize a few of these items, but they were so good they are worth repeating.

In the interests of space, the descriptions are also brief. Please contact me if you want additional information or clarification. I suggest that as you read through these ideas, you try to pick up the spirit behind them. Then see what you might be able to do to make your own operation more guest-friendly.

A note of caution: Even the best trick in the world will not make guests feel delighted unless you are sincerely doing it for their enjoyment and benefit. People can tell when they are being treated mechanically or when someone is applying a technique. Most patrons will probably find that sort of treatment to be impersonal at best and insulting at worst. If you can't have fun and make it a game to "wow" your guests, don't even try it!

Your patrons are worth it, and you will find it is a lot of fun for you and your staff besides!

12

Operating Policies

There are many delightful practices that arise in the moment out of a sincere desire to make the guests experience something extraordinary. Many others, however, can only come with the prior consent of management. In fact, the primary bottleneck to guest delight is probably in the executive office where the concern is often more with reducing costs than with increasing frequency and loyalty.

Here are a few policies to ponder that will bring back far more than they cost:

Complimentary umbrellas in inclement weather   Is the weather in your part of the planet a bit unpredictable? Is it possible that diners could arrive umbrella-less and coatless in the sunshine only to watch the heavens open and the rain pour down? What do you imagine the impact of this scene would have on your guests' sense of well-being? The solution is to get some big golf umbrellas and offer them to your guests to help them get to their cars (or even to their offices) without getting drenched.

Free food or beverages during the wait   I remember when the Pacific Cafe opened in San Francisco. It was out toward the beach, not a particularly prime location, and the weather was often cold and foggy. It was a small restaurant and had no place inside for guests to wait. One night shortly after they opened, the manager saw a waiting line extending down the sidewalk. Feeling sorry that his guests had to wait in the cold, he offered free wine to everyone until they could be seated. Needless to say, the waiting patrons loved it and didn't mind the wait anymore. The word spread quickly. The next night there was another line, the manager gave away more wine, and a tradition had been established. The waiting line (and the complimentary wine) continues to this day. The restaurant has given away a lot of wine . . . and they have also sold a lot of dinners!

When you are in Chicago, be sure to go to Lou Mitchell's for breakfast. You will probably have to wait a few minutes because it seems like there has been a waiting line at Lou Mitchell's for over 40 years! However, when they cannot seat you immediately, they still take care of you. Women will get a small box of Milk Duds. Men can't have Milk Duds. Men get donut holes. Children get a free banana.

Free newspapers or magazines   The longer people have to wait with nothing to do, the grumpier they will get. Is it worth a newspaper to keep them in a better mood? Coffee houses have seen the value of a magazine rack for mid-afternoon patrons. At the least, have a place to (neatly) stack newspapers left by other guests for the benefit of diners who come in later.

Free local phone calls   Guests appreciate making local calls without having to part with a pocketful of change, particularly as phone rates rise. While pay phones may provide a small source of revenue, you will make more money by giving people a reason to patronize your restaurant more often. Free local phones can be a point of difference in the market. The gesture is even more appreciated if the phones are on the tables.

Owner or manager on the floor   Train your staff and let them be stars. Even with a room full of stars, be sure to spend more time on the floor talking with your guests than in your office pushing paper. There is no substitute for personal presence and proprietary interest. Everybody enjoys knowing "the boss."

Something for nothing   Everybody loves something for nothing. Upscale restaurants do not have an exclusive hold on this touch. When you have breakfast at Lou Mitchell's in Chicago, you get a little fresh fruit that you didn't order when you are seated. Halfway through the meal they bring a little frozen yogurt sundae with fresh strawberries. A palate cleanser—at breakfast! I was impressed. Mike Hurst, owner of 15th Street Fisheries restaurant in Fort Lauderdale, regularly gives out free samples of potential new menu items. His guests are delighted.

Giving something for nothing is a wonderful gesture of hospitality. It helps your patrons try something new and gives them something to talk about. It also provides a marvelous start to what could otherwise look like a routine dining experience!

Free meals   What? Now you are thinking that I have really lost touch with reality, right? This idea may not be as insane as it sounds. When Phil Romano opened the first Macaroni Grill outside San Antonio, he wanted to increase dinner business early in the week. His solution was to give away all the meals on a Monday or Tuesday night! He only did it a few times, but the word quickly spread and the place was packed on Mondays and Tuesdays because "this might be the night!" Apparently the chance for a free meal was more intriguing than a guaranteed percentage off that you would get from a coupon.

Do you have a meal period when you would like to increase business? How much would it cost you to give away all the meals one day? How much advertising could you buy for that amount? How much exposure could you obtain by giving away the meals?

Now there are a number of ways to give away meals. You could have a fishbowl drawing where the guests draw a slip of paper at the end of the meal to find out what they get. The first few times you do it, have a disproportionate number of free meal tickets in there. You can then adjust the mix of rewards (free meals, free desserts, 50% off and so forth) to any ratio you want. You could just make a random management decision or give your staff the OK to comp a certain number of meals.

I would not suggest you advertise the policy—let the message be carried by word-of-mouth. You at least need to tell your guests whatever it is that you want them to tell others ("Isn't this fun? We do this every Monday and Tuesday night. Come back next week, you might be lucky again"). When you give away a meal, you might also approach the table with a line like, "Your dinner tonight came to $50. If you will take care of your server, I will take care of your meal." This will let them know what you did for them and help assure that the servers will not be penalized for your decision.

Reading material for single diners   Solo diners do not have the conversation of dining companions to occupy their time during lulls in the meal. Often they will bring a newspaper, book, or office work with them. If you attract (or want to attract) single diners, have reading material available and train your staff to offer it politely.

Free postcards and postage   Are you in a resort area? If so, consider printing up some postcards with a great photo of your restaurant on the front. Offer the cards to waiting guests. If they are on vacation, they will have the obligatory "wish you were here" cards to send, so why not have them send out ads for your restaurant? While they are waiting, they can take care of their social obligations and the time will pass more quickly. The postcard itself is an unexpected touch, but if you want to make it particularly delightful, offer to mail the cards for them. Stamps are less expensive (and personal endorsements are more powerful) than display ads.

Guests' names on reader boards   People love to see their names up in lights and you could give them their 15 minutes of fame. You have as much to gain by using your reader board to make your guests feel special as you do by using it to advertise your specials. When guests make a reservation, ask if they are celebrating a special occasion. If so, see if they would mind if you put it on the reader board. You could easily become *the* place in town to celebrate!

Pleasant surprises   The staff at a McGuffey's Restaurant in North Carolina had some time on their hands one day. Their solution was to wash the cars in the parking lot while their diners were having lunch! Can you imagine how much goodwill you would create by an unexpected gesture like this? What is the potential for taking the sting out of waiting in line at a fast food drive-up window by washing guests' cars? You could have a school group do the work as a fundraiser except that *you* pay them for each car washed, not the guest. You could even get a few points just by cleaning windshields!

"Rainy day rules"   My first restaurant, Crisis Hopkins, was in the financial district of San Francisco. We had a line out the door at lunch every day, but when it rained, people were more inclined to eat in their office building cafeteria rather than venture out in the weather. Lunch sales really dropped when it rained . . . and it rained fairly regularly from October to March. My approach was to establish what I called "rainy day rules." When it was raining, wine or dessert was free with lunch! It didn't take too long before weather stopped having a major impact on our volume. We gave away some wine but we sold a lot of lunches, too! In fact, people would often call to see if rainy day rules were in effect before they headed out.

Free seconds   I would rather give free seconds than to serve oversized portions initially. The food stays hotter, the waste is reduced, and it allows you to make a personal (and probably unexpected) offer to the guest. When was the last time a server asked you if she could bring you another serving of pot roast?

Pad and pencil by telephones   When people are on the phone, they often have to make notes. Have some note pads and golf pencils (with your logo, address, and phone on them, of course) by the phones to make it easier for your guests. The pads can also work well at the table for taking notes during business discussions. Your hope, of course, is that the guests will take the pad back to the office with them and have a constant reminder of your restaurant on their desk!

Free refills on soft drinks   Most restaurants give unlimited refills on coffee and iced tea. Why not do the same with soft drinks? Guests, particularly teenagers, will appreciate the gesture. David Setzer of Nickel City Cafe in Buffalo found that when he was giving unlimited refills, consumption averaged about 20 ounces per person. When he started putting a 16-ounce carafe on the table, guests would finish the carafe and be very content. His diners also liked the fact that they did not have to wait for refills. The practice reduced consumption and minimized running for his servers while increasing guest satisfaction—delightful!

Reserving entrees   Even if you do not take reservations, you could still allow guests to make a reservation for their entree. This is particularly nice when you have a fresh product that is in limited supply and in high demand. Clue your phone people in to this idea. If a guest asks about whether you have a particular item available that night, offer to reserve one for them (and then make sure that you do it!).

House charge accounts   This practice can be fraught with peril but it is a delightful perk for regular guests. Even if you do not want to get into the receivables business, you could make prior arrangements that would allow a guest to simply sign the check (and look very important to their dining companions). You would then add a tip and charge the meal to their credit card. It takes a little extra work on your part but it is a small price to pay for guest loyalty.

"The answer is yes. What's the question?"   If you want to eliminate most guest relations problems before they start, adopt this simple management policy long championed by "Coach" Don Smith. It is a simple way to say that the guest is always right, even when she is wrong. It acknowledges that you can never win an argument with a guest. It keeps the emphasis on assuring that guests have an enjoyable experience in your restaurant. What have you got to lose but unhappy patrons?

Social consciousness   Concern for the environment is increasing and restaurants are the target of criticism from many consumer groups. If you are not part of the solution, you are part of the problem. Recycle whatever you can and reduce your use of chemicals. Get your staff involved in finding ways to be more responsive to environmental concerns. Let your guests know that you care and are doing something to help. It can't hurt.

Conspicuous support of local charities   Be a good citizen. Your success comes from the support of your local community. If you only *take* from the people and never give anything back, you will look like an opportunist. Share your success and you will attract more of it. What goes around, comes around.

Free coffee for breakfast guests who have to wait   If you can get someone's day off to a good start, you have done them a real favor. Timing is critical during the breakfast period, so anything you can do to make a delay less painful is a good move. Offering free coffee to a guest who has to wait is a small gesture that will yield big returns in guest satisfaction.

Striking logo used tastefully   Image is everything. Look at the impact the Hard Rock Cafe has created from the widespread use of its logo! Create a distinctive logo. The more times you can put it in front of your guests, the more they will associate the image with the quality of their experience. This can work to your benefit if guests are enjoying themselves.

AV aids for business meetings   Do you want to be able to book business meetings to fill in those dead mid-morning and mid-afternoon periods in the middle of the week? To be more business-friendly, invest in a good quality screen and overhead projector and be sure to let your business clientele know about it. Making it easier for the meeting planner is a nice thing to do.

Cookbook   Many restaurants are finding that producing a cookbook is a great way to promote their businesses. It allows you to tell a lot of stories about the history of the restaurant, source of your recipes, and a number of other talking points that we will discuss in more detail later in this book. Instead of giving away product when there is a problem at the table, you can give a cookbook. The perceived value may be greater and the cost may be less!

Singing servers   If it fits with the concept of your restaurant, servers who sing or otherwise perform are definitely something different! If you are located in an area with an abundance of struggling actors, singers, or dancers, this can be a good way to solve your labor needs and showcase the talents of your staff. Staffing gets more complicated when you have to allow for performance time and exceptionally talented staff are likely to leave more quickly, but it can be an arrangement where everybody benefits.

Free (nonalcoholic) drinks for the designated driver Liquor liability and state-imposed DUI levels are putting more pressure on operators to operate responsibly. In most cases, the best defense is a good offense—demonstrating that your policies, procedures, and training are such that lapses are unlikely. To encourage responsible consumption of alcohol, your support of a designated driver program can be a factor in your favor. Where there is a designated driver there is usually a group of drinkers. Give away a few soft drinks and gain the business of the rest of the party.

On-time reservations   Guests make reservations at 7:00 p.m. because they want to eat at 7:00 p.m. You probably have a few minutes of grace, but people will not be pleased if they have to wait. Your job is to find a way to operate that allows you to keep your tables full and still honor reservations on time. As you are seating them (on time!), be sure to remind the guests that at your restaurant, 7:00 means 7:00. They will remember that the next time they go to a competitor and are left stewing in the bar.

One more idea: How about a policy that if you cannot seat people within 3 minutes of their reservation time, you will buy them a round of appetizers and their drinks will be free until you can get them to the table! That will keep your feet to the fire and help keep the guests happy.

Patron pagers   Vibrating pagers are a nice way to allow guests to wander while waiting for their tables, particularly if your restaurant is located in a shopping area, marina, or historic district. Typically the guest will leave a credit card or driver's license when he receives the pager and the greeter will signal the guest several minutes before the table is ready. The challenge here is to keep the personal nature of the exchange. The pagers should be offered as an option and not as a requirement. If people feel like they are being dismissed, the pagers will have a negative effect. Guests who prefer to wait in the restaurant should still be notified personally when their tables are ready.

Sparkling clean dining rooms and restrooms   Your guests expect your restaurant to be clean. When you surpass *clean* and make your restaurant *sparkle*, you improve your score and put your guests in a better mood. Sparkling facilities help make up for any lapses in the operation and give you a reputation for spotlessness.

Finding a seat for guests who have to wait   When guests have to wait, too often we just point them in the direction of the lounge and let them go. Consider having one of your staff escort them to a place where they can wait comfortably. It may be in the bar or just a spot in your waiting area. This offers one more chance to sell the wait, offer drinks or appetizers, and reinforce your commitment to guest service.

Opening the front door for guests   Olive Garden, the Italian dinner-house chain, has a staff person whose job is to greet guests enthusiastically and open the door for them. Christopher's in Phoenix goes one step farther: Their captains are required to walk guests to the valet stand to wait for their cars. They report it is an excellent way to provide personal service and find out what guests *really* thought of the evening.

13

Unexpected Touches

If the name of the game is to exceed guests' expectations, what better way to do that than to provide some pleasant surprises? I think back to one of the first Japanese cars I ever drove. There was a rest for my left foot, a place to put change, a slot for sunglasses, and a number of little creature comforts the makers of my old Chevy never even thought of. I was thrilled!

Very often, the most impactful touches are the small ones that eliminate a small irritation. Here are a few examples.

Hooks to hold purses   It is a busy Friday night and the bar is packed. The floor is covered with beer and you are feeling great at the early register readings! In the middle of this madness, where does a woman put down a $200 Coach bag? She cannot put it on the floor, there may not be any seats, and a tabletop may be out of the question. My solution was to mount little locker hooks under the bar top and under the tables. This provided a safe place to hang the bag and kept it off the floor so no one would trip over it. This can be a delightful touch and a reason for diners to think of you when they go to a competitor, reach under the table for the hook, and find only hardened chewing gum!

Calculator with the check   Parties of singles with a common check especially appreciate this touch. Groups of women also seem driven to create a painstakingly equitable cost split. Even if there is no entree cost to divide, many people appreciate a little help with calculating a tip. Credit card-sized calculators are inexpensive and easy to attach to a tray or check folder. It creates another point of difference and is worth considering.

Tables in the kitchen   A table by the kitchen door is the last place people want to sit, but a table in the kitchen itself commands a premium price. What a treat to eat in the kitchen and watch the controlled madness of a restaurant in mid-rush! Operators who have done this report the table is booked months in advance!

Many require that the chef work out a special menu for the group and even when the meals come at top dollar, guests line up to experience this unique dining environment!

FAX directions to first-time guests   Nobody likes to get lost or not know exactly where they are going. When a guest asks for directions to the restaurant, ask if they have a fax machine. If so, fax them a map that will show them exactly how to find you. You might also want to include a coupon on the fax page as an additional thank-you gesture.

Candle on the dessert tray   Most dessert trays, no matter how attractive the plates, are still a little flat and lifeless. Particularly in the evening, the desserts can be a little hard to see. For a more festive touch, simply put a small candle on the tray.

"Throwed rolls"   Lambert's Cafe in Sikeston, Missouri has a reputation for "throwed rolls," a unique way of passing out the bread! This unique touch, which started by accident on a busy night many years ago, has become a trademark of the restaurant that has garnered media attention from all over the world.

Interesting water pitcher   Restaurants in the Red Lion Hotels use an interesting ceramic water pitcher shaped like a fish. Because they are located primarily in the Pacific Northwest where salmon is king, it reinforces the regional theme and provides a unique twist to something as mundane as filling a glass of water.

"It's kissing time"   There is a restaurant in Portland, Oregon, called Portofino, presided over by Carlo, the stereotypical Italian restaurant owner. When guests enter the dining room, Carlo raps on his glass to get everyone's attention, introduces the newly arrived patrons to the other diners and, with a smile, raises a wine glass and says, "Ladies and gentlemen, it's kissing time!" Everyone toasts the new diners, kisses, and goes back to their dinners. Few people have the personality to pull this off, but it might be something worth pondering for an intimate little restaurant. (PS: If you are having a secret affair, I do not recommend you go to dinner at Portofino!)

Fresh flowers for the ladies   Flowers are always a special touch. Many restaurants offer flowers for special occasions like

Mother's Day or Secretaries Week. Others do it more regularly. What is appropriate will depend on the type of restaurant you have, but free flowers can be a delightful gesture in almost any restaurant at one time or another.

Small spoons for sugar   This is such a small touch but it shows an attention to detail that many guests will find delightful. Instead of a crock crammed full of sugar packets, how about a bowl of sugar with a small spoon in it. I am suggesting something smaller than a teaspoon—a spoon specifically for the sugar. Later in this part of the book I suggest providing smaller flatware for small children, so perhaps the scaled-down spoons could work here as well.

Staff names on menu   When you go to a movie, you get a complete list of all the people who had a part in making the picture. Why not provide similar credits on your menu, at least for your key people? The wine list could include the name of the cellar manager. The chef's name could appear on the menu. The pastry chef might get credit on the dessert menu. Particularly when so many of these people are never seen by the diners, it can be a nice touch that will instill pride and increase a sense of personal responsibility.

Golf cart in parking lot   Regas Restaurant in Knoxville has a huge parking lot and an older clientele. They have a golf cart patrolling the lot to bring people to and from their cars. This is appreciated any time, but particularly when the weather is less than ideal.

House camera   If people are celebrating a special occasion, it is always nice to have a commemorative photo. If the guests do not bring their own camera, why not have an instant camera in the house to handle the task? The photo will be a nice reminder of the restaurant.

Deliveries through the front door   A restaurant in Newport, Rhode Island, was in the middle of the summer dinner rush. Guests were standing around everywhere and the parking lot was snarled. The fish delivery was late and by the time the truck arrived, it could not get to the back of the restaurant. The driver asked the owner what to do with the 90-pound tuna he had on the truck. Thinking for a second, the owner told him to bring it in through the front door. With a lot of "excuse mes" two men held the huge fish over their heads and worked their way through the crowd into the kitchen. There was no need to make the point about fresh tuna that night!

Kid wrangler   If you have a lot of preteen children in the restaurant, you know how bored they can get. How about a person whose job it is to make the meal work for disenchanted children— what I would call a kid wrangler? With the parents' permission, they could round up a group of kids and take them for a tour of the restaurant. It would give the parents some peace and make the kids feel special. If the children are happy, the parents are happy!

Scissors for French onion soup   I have always wanted to serve French onion soup with a pair of scissors to clip off the cheese as you raise the spoon! It just seems like such a civilized idea! If any reader implements this idea, please let me know!

Upside-down Christmas tree   Hap Gray owns the Watermark Restaurant in Cleveland. Because floor space is tight, he was wondering how to handle the traditional Christmas tree as he approached his first holiday season. His solution was to decorate the tree and hang it upside down from the ceiling. It has been a tradition ever since and his guests would never forgive him if he changed the practice!

Recipe cards   If a guest compliments you on a particular dish, wouldn't she be thrilled if you gave her the recipe? In the Intermountain West, a coffee shop chain called 4B's is noted for their tomato soup. Instead of keeping this recipe a secret, they provide free recipe cards to any guest who is interested. The item is such a signature that competitors would be hard-pressed to steal it and I doubt if many guests actually make the soup. It is, however, an interesting reminder of their meal and something to talk about.

Free cherrywood and recipe   Sharp's Fresh Roaster in Seattle takes the recipe card idea one step farther. On each table they place a small bag of cherrywood chips and a recipe for smoked cherrywood chicken. Even if the guests try the recipe, they may just be reminded of how much work is involved in the item and how much better they do it at Sharp's!

Menus in foreign languages   You would never offer English-speaking guests a menu written in Chinese, yet many operators think nothing of presenting an English language menu to a Chinese-speaking guest. It is only courteous to give your guests menus they can understand. Ask your multilingual guests to help you translate your menu into other languages (it gets them more personally involved with you). Include English subtitles so your staff can follow along. It is a small gesture of respect for a small segment of your market but a true measure of your passion for guest gratification.

Selection of reading glasses   It's hell when you pass 40! For your guests who need a little optical help and have forgotten their reading glasses, have a selection on hand to help them out. Inexpensive reading glasses in standard prescriptions are readily available in most pharmacies. Present the selection in a good-looking lined wooden box. Your guests will appreciate and remember this unexpected amenity.

Selection of sunglasses   When the weather is good, seating on an outside deck is a treat. The problem is that the sun can be pretty intense and make the experience a strain. Why not have a box of sunglasses to loan to diners on the deck? The cost is minimal and the offer of some sun protection is an unexpected surprise. My second restaurant had a deck. I found that many guests left their own sunglasses at the table anyway and never bothered to return for them. When that happens, add them to the box!

Different color mugs for regular/decaf   I drink decaffeinated coffee and it seems like servers are always trying to pour regular coffee into my cup. I always have to be on the lookout for the coffee pot swooping in from my blind side and it takes my attention away from enjoying the meal. Many restaurants put a small coaster under the cups of decaf, but that is not always so obvious. McGuffey's Restaurants in the southeast solved this problem simply by having two different coffee mugs—white for regular and brown for decaf (or is it the other way around?). In any case, it is immediately obvious to the server who is drinking what.

Finger bowls or hot towels   One of the nicest traditions in Japanese dining is the hot towels at the beginning of the meal. Even airlines offer this touch in the first class cabin. It is a pleasant gesture that can work in many other venues as well. All it takes is some rolled washcloths and a little hot water. A squeeze of lemon is a nice enhancement. South Street Smokehouse in Nashville keeps them ready to go in a hot well at the service stand. I would also offer the towels at the end of the meal, particularly if the menu includes items that might be eaten with the fingers.

14

Special Occasions

When it is time to celebrate a special occasion, people automatically think about going out to dinner. It behooves every operator to make sure that going out to celebrate is a positive and truly memorable experience. The occasion is different from a routine dinner out and it should be handled differently.

Whether your approach is subtle or effusive, give some thought to what you can to do to make special occasions more special. Here are a few ideas to get you started.

Sing a song other than "Happy Birthday to You"   Show a little originality! The traditional birthday song is what your competitors sing and your guests are immune to it. Get their attention with something short and personalized to your restaurant. Make it a song that your staff enjoys singing. It is unsettling to see people singing if their hearts aren't in it. If you do it well, they will think of your restaurant for their next special occasion. As an alternative the staff at the Crow's Nest in Venice, Florida offers a rendition of the traditional birthday tune played on kazoos!

Toast to people celebrating special occasions   For more upscale operations, there is an alternative to the often-annoying practice of singing to guests. Rap on a glass to get the attention of the room and propose a toast, "To Mickey and Sylvia on the occasion of their thirtieth anniversary. May you have another 30 years together!" Everyone raises their glasses to acknowledge the couple, drinks a little, and the deed is neatly done.

Make a big deal of special occasions   Some places are better suited to going crazy with special occasions. The alternative to a low-key acknowledgment is to do something bold and brassy that pleasantly embarrasses the honorees.

For example, Azteca Restaurants in the Pacific Northwest have a huge sombrero (with Azteca on the front, of course) that they plunk on the head of people celebrating a birthday. The waiters sing (in Spanish) and someone snaps a Polaroid picture. The birthday celebrant is always grinning like a fool and the pictures are usually great! The restaurant slips the photo into a paper frame that is then signed by the members of the restaurant staff. Happy Birthday from your friends at Azteca!

Offer complimentary cakes   If someone is celebrating a birthday or anniversary, it is a nice touch to bring them a special little cake or some other special dessert. Some people will tell you it is a special occasion even when it isn't just to get the cake . . . but they still pay for their dinner and drinks!

Decorate the table   How about doing something special on the table itself for parties celebrating special occasions? Seattle-based Cucina! Cucina! will spread a little confetti, put out a few balloons, and toss a half dozen streamers across the table top. If you can put people in a festive mood from the time they are seated, they will have a more delightful experience and a more positive impression of your restaurant!

15

Service

Service is essentially a technical equation. It is about serving from the left and clearing from the right. It is about all tasks flowing smoothly together in the best interests of the guest. It is about what you do.

Hospitality, on the other hand, is a human equation. It is about how you deliver the elements of service and about how much guests feel you care about them when you do it. Even the best technical service will not be delightful if the guests do not sense that their well-being is foremost in your mind.

There are countless elements that comprise delightful service. Because so many of them are the direct responsibility of the service staff, I have included several ideas in Chapter 66 taken from my book for servers, *50 Tips to Improve Your Tips*. For now, here are a few more service-related suggestions.

Smiling eye contact   Nothing warms the heart like smiling eye contact. Coach your staff in the importance of starting the relationship with all new guests by looking them directly in the eye and giving them a big smile.

Move toward arriving guests   Hospitality is about your ability to establish a personal connection with your guests. To do that, you have to deal with your guests as individuals, not as customers. Get your greeters out from behind the podium. Better yet, get rid of the podium entirely. My idea of a great start to the meal is when guests walk through the door and someone is moving toward them with a smile. This does not require that the greeter be glued to the front door, just that someone maintain a sense of what is happening at the entry and head toward newly arriving guests as soon as they enter the restaurant.

Acknowledge newly arrived guests within 30 seconds
You have about 30 seconds from the time people walk in the door

to make eye contact and let people know that you know they are there. If you are in the middle of something, finish it up quickly and take care of the guests. If guests sense that they are important to you as soon as they walk in the door, they will be in a much better mood for the rest of the meal.

Offer smaller portions at smaller prices   Dieters and elderly diners appreciate this option and it can work to your advantage. You can offer half the portion for 60–75% of the menu price and still maintain respectable margins. This approach also allows entrees to be attractive as appetizers. Half-portions will also make you more attractive to the growing number of diners who prefer grazing to ordering a full meal.

Have the chef serve the meal   Every so often, when you are into the back side of the dinner rush, have the chef bring the food out and serve it. It will require a clean set of whites, of course, but imagine the reaction of a guest when the chef arrives at the table, presents the plate, and says, "I just made this for you. I hope you enjoy it!"

Offer pass-arounds   When you eat at Lambert's Cafe in Sikeston or Springfield, Missouri (the home of "throwed rolls"), people are always coming to the table offering items you didn't order— fried okra, macaroni and tomatoes, white beans, red pepper relish, and other goodies are all free! How could you benefit from an idea like this?

Pour the house wine   Typically, when a guest orders a glass of wine, it is poured at the bar and carried to the table. A nice touch is to bring the bottle and pour the wine at the table. It gives wines by the glass in general, and house wines in particular, a more respectful service.

Bring water to everyone at the table if one person asks for it   Water is an item that increasingly is served only upon request in many restaurants. If one person at the table orders water, it is safe to assume that everyone will want it, particularly if you forget to ask! Just make it a practice to bring water to everyone and save yourself some work!

High staff presence   There is something special about a person who is obviously thinking of nothing but your well-being. Your staff will follow your example. If you are distracted when you talk with them, they will be distracted when they talk to your guests. If you define the job of the manager as maintaining a positive climate in the restaurant, high staff presence will be more common. This notion is discussed in more detail in Chapter 57.

Use guest's names frequently   Nothing is more pleasant to people than the sound of their own name. Make it a game to find out the names of your guests and use them whenever appropriate during the meal. The greeter is in a perfect position to get the guests' names, either from the reservation list or just by asking them as they are seated. Remember always to use only their last name preceded by Mr. or Ms. until or unless they ask you to be less formal.

Cafeteria self-service   When I took over the foodservice program for the U.S. Olympic Training Centers, I inherited a standard military-type cafeteria operation. The athletes were fed but were not very excited. One of the first changes I made was to make the entire operation self-service, allowing the athletes to make their own selections. They could take as much (or as little) as they wanted. Some very unexpected things happened.

The first change I noticed was that the food cost per meal dropped almost 15%. When they could take whatever they wanted, the athletes took less food than we were giving them before. The most pleasant surprise, though, was the change in the relationship between my staff and the athletes. Freed from their serving duties, my crew's main job was to keep the line replenished and looking attractive. Their conversations with the athletes changed from task-oriented ("do you want peas?") to being more personal. Everybody had a more enjoyable time. This approach may not work for everyone, but it worked for our Olympic athletes!

16

Food and Beverage

For whatever key roles service and hospitality play in restaurant success, people still go out to eat and drink. Some of their expectations go without saying. They expect their food and drink to be prepared and handled in a safe manner, they expect to get what they ordered, they expect the hot food to be hot and the cold food to be cold, they expect what they ordered to look and taste like it did the last time they ordered it.

However, because so many operators seem to want to make things as easy as possible for themselves and do not consider the impact of their actions on their guests, there are many opportunities to give diners an unexpected treat. Here are a few of my favorites.

Unexpected touches   Find a way to do a better job with something ordinary. For example, when you order coffee at Hudson's Bar & Grill in San Luis Obispo, California, it comes with a cinnamon stick, chocolate chips, and fresh cream . . . and is priced like regular coffee! The advantage of making a point of difference out of a common item is that your guests will think of you the next time they dine at another restaurant.

Housemade croutons   Poor quality croutons out of a box can make guests forget an otherwise memorable salad. Croutons are easy to make and can be a point of difference in your salad presentation. Cut the bread cubes a little larger than normal. Toast the bread cubes in the oven, then sauté them quickly in olive oil and fresh garlic. Superb!

Interesting jams, jellies, or preserves   Most restaurants simply purchase jams, jellies, and preserves. If you make the product yourself, it brings a homey touch to your restaurant. You will enhance your image as a quality operation and gain a unique position in the market. Even if you buy the product from a local source, it will be superior to an institutionally prepared bulk product.

Exceptional, piping hot bread   Oh, the magic of fresh, hot bread! Nothin' says lovin' and all that. It is worth the effort to create a superior bread product and find a unique presentation for it. Every time your patrons eat in a competing restaurant, they will think of you when the bread arrives.

Signature items   To be successful in today's market, it takes more than just doing a good job. Be famous for something. Find items that you can do better than anyone else and use them to build your reputation.

Housemade desserts   Baking is a lost art at home. Exceptional signature desserts baked fresh on the premises are a major point of difference in the market. If you cannot bake your own desserts, personalize a purchased product with a signature sauce, fresh fruit, or something unusual. Don't just cut the cheesecake and put it on a plate.

After-dinner treat   People love pleasant surprises. Instead of ordinary mints with the check, how about a chocolate-covered strawberry, tartlet, or a fresh cookie? In Australia and New Zealand, it is common to receive a fresh chocolate with the coffee. See what you can come up with. Anybody can buy mints.

Garnished food pans on the buffet   Legendary restaurants garnish every food presentation to enhance its visual appeal for their guests. If you operate a cafeteria or buffet, you cannot garnish plates, but you *can* dress up the food display by garnishing the pans of hot food. Do an imaginative job of garnishing and you can soften your institutional image.

Unique regional or local products   In an age of homogenization, when every mall in the country has the same stores and the same chain restaurants appear on every corner, I believe there is an untapped longing for something honest. What can you offer that people cannot get anywhere else in the country? Lettuce from the farm down the road will always taste better than lettuce from the supermarket (but only if you let the guests know that you have used it).

Dessert samplers   One of Randy Rayburn's more successful offerings at the Sunset Grill in Nashville is the dessert sampler.

Guests can order smaller portions of three or ten different desserts attractively displayed on a mirror tray. He says that people love to have a choice and hate to make a decision, so diners who might otherwise say no to a single dessert will say yes to a sampler. An additional advantage is that guests get to try more of Sunset Grill's superb desserts and are more likely to order them the next time they come in.

Sizing appetizers to the size of the party   This is an unexpected personal touch that is so easy to do, yet few operators ever think to accommodate or suggest it. Let's say you have a party of four who order an appetizer that normally comes with three pieces. What would it take to offer to size it for four people, add an extra piece, and adjust the price accordingly? Whatever it takes, it is worth the effort to make your restaurant more guest-friendly. Besides, the personal awareness and concern for the guests inherent in the offer will delight your diners.

Organic produce   Produce grown without chemical fertilizers or insecticides is becoming more readily available and more reasonably priced. Often, it is a noticeably superior product. In some markets, organic produce can be an unexpected and welcome addition to the menu.

Unique butter   Diners expect butter to come with the bread and you should certainly see that they get it. However, in addition to regular butter, try a special butter that you make up yourself. The best blend would depend on what the butter will accompany, but I have seen honey butter, herb butter, dill butter, and tomato butter used effectively. At the best, it could become a signature item for you. At the worst, it will break the routine for your guests.

Housemade products   Even supporting items can help make you famous. You could cut your own french fries. You could make your own mayonnaise, applesauce, potato chips, pasta, ice cream, salad dressing, barbecue sauce, or desserts. Few restaurants can afford to prepare everything from scratch, but look at what you are using and see what items you could do in-house and make memorable points of difference.

Separate coaster for the bottle and the glass   Coasters or cocktail napkins keep the tabletop dry. Beer bottles sweat as much as glasses do. Your guests will appreciate your awareness that a wet table is an unpleasant experience.

Chilled mugs and glasses   Beverages stay colder in cold glasses. While the practice of chilled mugs for beer is not particularly unique any more, those who like their beer cold always appreciate the service. (Note: Don't keep beer glasses in the freezer. It frosts the mug but damages the product.) Many establishments chill wine glasses for white wine sold in the bar. You have nothing to lose by making the gesture.

Inventive garnishes   There are some cocktails where guest expectations will dictate a particular garnish. In other cases, you have more options. Experiment a little and see if you can find a fresh way to present some of your old favorites. How about a southwestern martini with a jalepeño pepper in it?

Exceptional bar snacks   If your establishment only serves alcohol, guests may not expect much creativity. If you are a full-service restaurant, though, you can use your bar snacks to display your culinary prowess and entice drinkers to stay for dinner. Go beyond what people expect. Years ago, Paoli's in San Francisco built one of the strongest happy hours in the city by offering a free buffet that would put most hotel brunches to shame. They gave away a lot of food . . . and they sold a lot of drinks! How many cocktail franks and cheese cubes can people eat?

Unusual glassware   Visual appeal is an important part of beverage presentation. Unusual glassware is an easy way to create a point of difference for your bar operation. Pat O'Brien's, the legendary New Orleans bar, merchandises their world-famous Hurricane by using a distinctive glass that becomes a souvenir of the restaurant.

Hors d'oeuvre with each drink   A hot hors d'oeuvre with each drink is a very European touch. If it fits with your concept, the hors d'oeuvre approach can showcase your kitchen and increase your bar sales. If you use the hors d'oeuvres to allow guests to sample items from your menu, you also can build your dinner sales. At the least, you will create a point of difference and build your reputation.

Logo on glassware   Very few establishments are willing to spend the money for personalized glassware, creating an open field for those who see the power of it. Custom crested glassware makes a memorable impact on the public. It adds variety and distinction to your beverage service. It also can be an effective advertising vehicle if you use it as a giveaway. Since some guests are going to steal your glasses anyway, you might as well get the promotional value!

Oversized wine glasses   There is something elegant about a large wine glass that makes people feel more like ordering wine. When I opened my first restaurant in San Francisco in the late 1970s, white wine was the drink of choice. All my competitors were serving 9 ounces of wine in a 10-ounce glass. We served 10 ounces of wine in a 17-ounce glass and promptly gained the patronage of most of the women in the Financial District! They loved the look and feel of the big glass. We also found we were less likely to spill the glasses while carrying drinks to the table through a crowded bar. Better yet, we sold 10 ounces of wine for 25% more than our competitors were getting for 9 ounces . . . and had better word of mouth and happier guests in the process!

Designated driver program   An important part of the sale of alcohol these days is to promote sensible consumption. If the industry does not take the lead to promote responsible drinking voluntarily, you can be sure some bureaucrat will dictate how we have to run our businesses. Large groups of people create energy and excitement in the bar. If you can help them have a good time and get home safely, they will be alive to patronize you again. Support responsible drinking by providing an incentive for groups to have a designated driver. Call a cab for any guest who may not be in a condition to drive home safely. Have the house pick up the cost of the ride. Remember that one alcohol-related accident can put you out of business.

Fresh-squeezed juices   In an era of reconstituted juices, you can create another point of difference by using fresh juices at the bar. It takes more work to make a screwdriver with fresh oranges, but imagine how distinctive the drink will be to the screwdriver fan! It is not practical to do *all* your juices to order. For example, it is almost impossible to make an acceptable tomato juice on the premises. Still, the exceptional freshness and merchandising value of squeezing juices to order can put your bar on the map.

Bottled mixers   Bottled mixers have a sharper carbonation than postmix soft drinks from a gun. This is particularly true of tonic water. Since most of your competitors use guns, consider making another distinction for your bar by featuring bottled mixers. Train your staff to tell guests of this special touch and your patrons will have something to talk about to their friends.

Individual coffee pots   One way to be sure guests don't have to wait for coffee is to give them a personal coffee pot. There are attractive carafes of all sizes and styles on the market at very reasonable prices. If you present them properly, carafes are a welcome touch, particularly in the morning.

Extensive alcohol-free selections   People drink to be sociable, not to get drunk. If you can extend the length of the social period, your sales will benefit. With the growing awareness of drinking and driving, it only makes sense to get creative with alcohol-free options.

Signature drinks   Success in today's market takes more than just pouring a good drink. Every bar in town can put out Chivas Regal on the rocks. If you want to be a legend and draw business, be famous for something. Find an item you can do better than anyone else in town and push it. Better yet, invent a drink your staff can honestly recommend when talking to your guests. Pat O'Brien's success in New Orleans attests to the power of a signature drink.

Extensive selection of wines by the glass   As the public becomes more aware of the dangers of drinking and driving, they are consuming smaller amounts of higher quality beverages. People who would have previously ordered a bottle of wine are showing particular interest in premium wines by the glass. You can easily take advantage of this trend. Some restaurants even offer individual glasses of most selections on their wine list. Wine lovers and would-be wine lovers will appreciate the opportunity to expand their wine experiences without having to buy a full bottle.

The more wines you have by the glass, the easier you make it for guests to upgrade their wine selections and sample new vintages. Sunset Grill has close to 300 wines on their list and Randy Rayburn says he will pour almost any of them by the glass if a guest requests it. Most restaurateurs would cringe at this idea, but Randy has a different outlook. "The way I see it," he says, "If we can't sell the remaining three glasses, we shouldn't be in the restaurant business!"

Premium well   Guests get nervous about brands of liquor they have never heard of. Why incur the expense of trying to have a bottle of every liquor in the world on hand, particularly when the majority hardly sell at all? A premium well may offer the solution to both problems. For example, instead of stocking seven medium-grade scotches, you might have Chivas Regal in the well with Glenlivet as a super premium upgrade. Few Dewar's drinkers will refuse Chivas Regal. A premium well simplifies inventories and provides a point of difference for your establishment. In most markets, you can charge more for the premium pour.

***Really* great coffee**   You have to have exceptional coffee. This has always been true, but as diners become more educated to the wonders of espresso, they are becoming more discriminating in their coffee tastes. Coffee is often the last product people have before they leave, and a substandard cup of coffee can take the glow off an otherwise outstanding evening.

Special iced tea   Consider offering a special iced tea as well. There are now tea blends specially formulated to hold up well to ice. Check out herbal teas and spiced teas to see what might work for you. It is an easy way to upgrade an otherwise mundane product. While we are talking about iced tea, be sure the product you offer is exceptional, even if it is not particularly different. There is a noticeable difference between brewed tea and the freeze-dried product. Tea that is refrigerated overnight will become cloudy. Pay attention to the small points . . . your guests do.

Bottled water   I am seeing more and more restaurants offering a selection of bottled waters on their menus. This may be in reaction to the generally declining rate of alcohol consumption or it could be playing to the water snobs, but having more nonalcoholic choices cannot hurt. Besides, you won't be able to get much money for a glass of tap water!

Carafe service   Any item that you would automatically refill can be presented in a carafe. Water, iced tea, soft drinks, and coffee could all be left on the table, allowing the guests to refill their own glasses without having to wait for a server to do it. Carafe service does not have to be boring. The Villa in Palmer Lake, Colorado, a romantic Italian restaurant, presents water in a beautiful pressed glass bottle. It is just tap water, but the candlelight flickering through the bottles on the table adds another dimension to the look of the dining room.

Place to put the spoon when coffee is served in a mug
My wife is very fastidious when it comes to cleanliness. She does not trust tabletops to be clean enough to eat from and this extends to where to put the spoon after she stirs her coffee. When coffee is served in a cup and saucer, no problem. When coffee is served in a mug, however, it gets trickier. If you use mugs, be aware of this sensitivity and bring a side plate when you bring the sugar and cream. Someone will be delighted!

Extensive dessert wine selection   Consider adding a selection of dessert wines to your menu. They satisfy the need for sweetness, are an interesting alternative to cordials, and can be a workable alternative for guests who do not order dessert. As the market develops, so does the variety of wines available, many of which are truly surprising. When you can turn your guests on to something new and wonderful, it makes them feel like pioneers, gives them something to tell their friends about, and establishes more of a personal connection with your restaurant.

Regional beers and wines   As a constant traveler, I always appreciate the chance to sample regional specialties. The boom in microbreweries has re-energized the beer market, and more regions of the country are discovering that they can produce wines of reasonable quality. Educating guests to unique regional products can make the evening more memorable and help support local producers.

Wines by the glass, taste, or percentage consumed   I was delighted when I first saw this idea at Le Central in Denver. Billed as "the affordable French restaurant," Le Central will sell you wine by the glass. They will sell you wine by the taste. I had seen both those formats before, but they also offered something I had never seen a restaurant do before—they would sell you wine based on the percentage of the bottle that you consumed! I questioned the idea initially, but could not see a particular health department problem unless someone drank from the bottle! The more I thought about it, the more I liked the idea.

For my wife, a glass of wine is a lot (and finishing the rest of the bottle is less fun for me than it used to be), so a bottle of wine is really too much for the two of us. When we are out with another couple, one bottle is not quite enough and we would get caught in the "do we or don't we" debate on the second bottle. This policy would avoid both problems . . . and make your bottle of Mondavi different from your competitor's bottle of Mondavi. You might want to keep control of the bottle and your liquor laws may or may not address this issue, but this is an idea worth considering.

Coasters instead of cocktail napkins   Particularly in the summer when glasses of iced beverage sweat so profusely, cocktail napkins turn to pulp quickly. Consider using a fiber coaster instead. It will hold up better and can be a valuable souvenir of your restaurant. In fact, I would encourage guests to take a few home with them. I would even drop off a supply of my coasters to owners of vacation rental units in the area!

Beer served in buckets of ice   I first saw this idea in Mexico and I like it. Any beer drinker knows that the only way to have an ice cold beer is to have the beer on ice. For reasons I still do not totally understand, a refrigerator just will not get the brew as chilled. The bucket is also a perfect way to keep the unpoured beer cold until you are ready to drink it.

Extensive beer selection   Beer tastes are becoming more discerning. In addition to the wide range of imported beers, there are also more and more domestic microbrews. To delight the beer drinkers, give them lots of different brews to sample! Several years ago, Marv Hunt, then the beverage manager at C. I. Shenanigan's in Spokane, Washington, increased the number of taps from 7 to two dozen, 21 of which were local and regional microbrews. Draft beer sales increased by 60% and became the largest contributor to the profitability of the bar operation.

Complimentary tastes of wine   If you want to sell wine, guests have to know what they are buying. Many are quite sophisticated and others are just learning. You know how difficult it is to stay current on wines! If a guest has a question about a particular wine, offer them a taste to help them reach a decision.

Extensive heart-healthy menu options   While this trend is still in its infancy, there is a real opportunity to gain a controlling position in the market. With the right recipes, food items, and equipment, you can prepare low-fat dishes that are as tasty as any conventional offering. Of course, not all selections have low-fat versions, but you might be surprised at what is possible by modifying recipes and preparation methods. For example, I have designed a well-balanced restaurant menu where 75% of the items meet American Heart Association standards . . . including hamburgers and french fries! All it takes is wanting to do it.

Imaginative dessert selections   There is always room for dessert. It is only the *idea* of dessert that gives guests pause. It is interesting that many diners will carefully order low-calorie entrees and follow up with a massive dessert! You can most always sell a dessert for two diners to split, provided you capture their imagination.

To do this, offer some signature desserts—items so unique and mouth-watering that your diners just can't refuse. Present them either in person with a dessert tray or in heartfelt word pictures. Assume that nobody can pass up your fresh peach cobbler. It helps if you make your desserts on the premises instead of purchasing them from outside sources. Back all this up with an attractive dessert menu. Since most people don't bake exotic desserts at home, you can offer your guests something truly special that they can't get anywhere else.

17

Teens

Y ou can love them or you can hate them, but you cannot deny
that teenagers are your future consumers. They may even be
a big part of your business already. Teens are at the age when they
develop the habits that will carry them into adulthood. If you understand their needs and treat them well, dining in your restaurant
could be a habit that stays with them for years.

If you need a more immediate incentive, here are a few more
points to ponder. In most families, the teenagers are the ones who
decide where the family goes out to dinner. Parents often make
calculating the tip an exercise in practical mathematics, so teens
often decide how much of a tip the family will leave. Teenagers will
patronize your restaurant with their parents, in groups with their
peers, or on dinner dates. Each situation has slightly different
problems and opportunities.

Don't make the mistake of treating teenagers like children. They
are as aware and observant as any adult diners. Today's teenagers
have extensive dining-out experience in a wide range of restaurants. They have their own opinions about things and you may be
surprised at what they like and dislike about restaurants. Here are
some positive ideas.

Free gum after the meal   You give mints to the adults after the
meal, why not give gum to teenagers? If you really want to make
some points, make it bubble gum! You probably want to make it
sugarless to keep the parents happy and, yes, you are going to be
scraping some of it out from under your tables . . . but you will be
doing that anyway!

Bottled sodas   As you might expect, teens are connoisseurs of
soft drinks. They appreciate the sharper carbonation of bottled
sodas over the postmix product.

Something to look at   Teens thrive on visual activity and
enjoy having something to look at. They like restaurants that have

"a lot of junk" on the walls, television sets, windows on the street—anything that is highly visual.

Souvenirs   Teens will prize keepsake glasses with your restaurant's logo. They are collectors and look for places where they can add to their accumulation of memorabilia. Tie the glass in with a signature drink that enhances your establishment's image (and profitability).

Free beverage refills   Adolescents have a continual thirst. They appreciate restaurants that recognize this need with prompt (free) beverage refills. The initial price of the drink is only a partial consideration. You will gain points by charging a little more for a drink and giving free refills. (This is a nice touch for adults, as well!) You can do even better by making the cup a souvenir of your restaurant.

Unusual desserts   Teenage guests love anything sweet. They are enthusiastic to find a restaurant with many different desserts from which to choose. Offer interesting desserts with clever names and you will increase your teen patronage as you build your dessert sales.

Cool t-shirts   The Hard Rock Cafe is a definite stop for teenagers because they have a distinctive t-shirt that everybody wants. There are many other examples of restaurants that have built their fame with a distinctive logo and a well-merchandised line of clothing. Eskimo Joe's in Stillwater, Oklahoma, even has a four-color, 28-page clothing catalog published twice a year. If you want teenagers to think about your restaurant, get a great t-shirt.

Mocktails   Don't automatically assume that teens only want soft drinks. They love the idea of having a range of beverage choices as diverse as that available to your adult diners. The same alcohol-free signature items that appeal to adults can give teenage diners a new range of beverage choices.

Sensitivity to conversational stalemates   When teenage couples go out for dinner, they often find themselves caught in a socially awkward situation when nobody at the table can think of anything to say. I'm sure you can remember these uncomfortable social deadlocks when you were growing up. Be sensitive to this situation and stop by the table to make a comment or suggestion when you sense that conversation at the table has reached an impasse. Your presence will loosen up the situation and make all your young guests more comfortable.

Exhibition cooking   Young diners are very sensitive to how you prepare their food. They are also curious about what the process looks like. Exhibition kitchens are a real attraction. If you sense that your teenage diners are restless (and if your layout permits), offer them a quick tour of the restaurant. They soak up new experiences like a sponge. You can use the excursion to point out what makes your restaurant different from your competition. Educate them about what they should be looking for when they go to restaurants. Teens love to have something to tell their friends about. It can't hurt to have them talking about what a great restaurant you have.

Attentive, respectful service   In the end, teenagers just want the same responsive service that any other guest expects. They don't want to be treated like children or second-class citizens. They appreciate friendly staff who show a genuine concern for their well-being and enjoyment.

18

Families

Families with children can be a profitable source of business for many restaurants, not just those who focus on the family. The trick in developing this market segment lies with understanding what they want and taking care of the details.

When dealing with families, it helps to understand that adults and children view dining in two different ways. For adults, meals are a social experience. Adults come to restaurants for conversation and to enjoy the company of their companions. Children's lives revolve around play and meals are mostly a biological function ("I'm hungry, feed me." "I'm full, now what?"). Serving the family effectively means addressing both needs. Let the children be children while their parents enjoy their meals in a more leisurely manner.

Here are a few ideas to make the dining experience more delightful for both groups.

Wet towels or wetnaps   Children's hands are always dirty. If you provide a way to clean sticky hands at the table, you will win the undying appreciation of the parents. It's hard enough to take a group of children out to eat without having to shuttle them to the restrooms for a cleanup. The solution can be as easy as packaged Wet-Naps or as classic as warm, damp washcloths.

Stock of disposable diapers   Most parents come prepared, but if an emergency arises, it's hard to improvise. Have an assortment of disposables in different sizes and let the parents know with a sign in the restrooms. You will gain a few points for attention to detail even if they never take advantage of the offer.

Separate area for nursing   Knowing how you will handle this question when it comes up is important. Having a comfortable area set aside for nursing mothers is even better. Nursing babies in public is more common than it used to be. Still, it can be a delicate situation for both the mother and your other guests. (It does not bother the baby, I suspect!) If possible, a separate room with a comfortable armchair will resolve the situation to everyone's delight.

Routinely (and quickly) check for forgotten articles   It is not that the family will never recover the lost items. It is more a recognition that families don't need the inconvenience of having to return for forgotten items. They will appreciate and remember that you found that favorite toy that rolled behind the plant before their youngster threw a tantrum about it!

High chairs on wheels   Particularly in restaurants where the parents have to wait in line for their food, rolling high chairs by the front door are a definite plus. Parents can place their small children in the chair and keep them under control while waiting and all the way to the table.

Stands for infant carriers   Molded infant carriers are becoming more common. Unfortunately, they don't usually fit on chairs. They are dangerous to put on the floor and awkward on top of the table. You can buy stands that attach to a high chair and hold infant carriers securely. They are worth a look.

"Give 'em!"   Children love gifts. A memento of their meal (and of your restaurant) can do wonders for developing loyalty in the younger set. Call it bribery if you like, but it works!

Smaller flatware for small children   Do you really want to be child-friendly? Have special flatware for children! When you consider that children are much smaller than adults (duh!!), you can see how difficult it is for a small child to successfully handle adult-sized utensils. This personal attention for your smallest patrons will thrill everyone at the table!

Smaller glassware for small children   The rationale here is the same, although it will probably not require a special purchase. Choose glasses with a smaller diameter and shorter height, even if that means bringing a carafe of the beverage for refills. It will make the meal more pleasant for everyone and save you a lot of spills.

Stuffed animals to "dine" with children   The Family Buggy in Livonia, Michigan has several large stuffed bears. When there are children at the table, they pull up an extra chair and bring over one of the bears to "dine" with the children. They started with one, immediately had to get a second, and probably have a third and fourth one by now. The kids are excited and the restaurant has a point of difference from competitors. They also sell the bears . . . to the grandparents . . . for $200!

Free balloons   I don't know what it is about balloons. Kids are fascinated by them. Maybe it is the fact that they float, but investing in a helium tank and a stock of balloons is a proven child-pleaser. If you have a unique balloon design with your logo on it, so much the better.

Balloon man   I was at Chevy's Restaurant in St. Louis on a Friday night and they had a balloon man making the rounds of the family tables. He was chatting with the children and making animals, hats, and other delights from long balloons. The children were thrilled, not only by the balloons, but by the personal attention. The adults appreciated the care directed toward their youngsters. The restaurant had happy guests. Everybody won.

Lego® table   Kids love Legos® or other similar building blocks. If you have an unproductive corner of the dining room, perhaps one with a "bad table" that irritates guests when they are seated there, consider converting it into a small play area for small children. The play area itself is delightful and the Lego® table is an easy way to occupy children.

Toy box   I know several restaurants that have a toy box at the entrance. When children come in to dine, they are allowed to select one toy from the box. It is theirs to play with until they leave. You can either purchase toys or collect them from your other diners, many of whom probably have a garage full of playthings from children long since grown. If you know a child has a particular favorite, you could offer to reserve it for them when their parents make the dinner reservation!

Special treats   If you do something for children that nobody else in town does, it is wonderful! It is as much about the personal attention as it is about the goodie itself, but think about it. How about a gingerbread man with the child's name on it in icing? Use your imagination.

Baby-sitting service   Some restaurants are offering what amounts to child care. The first one I saw was called "A Piece of Quiet" in Denver. There were two entrances. Parents dropped their kids in a separate dining area that had a special menu and an adult supervisor. While the children played, ate pizza, and watched videos, the adults dined in an adjacent restaurant. The children's area was visible through one-way glass between the rooms. Remember that once they have finished eating, children want to start doing something else. If you can provide a way to accommodate this, it is delightful!

Flex straws   Small children and tall glasses are a dangerous combination. Even drinking from a smaller glass can be a challenge for a small child with a straight straw. To make it easier, have a stock of flex straws for the little ones. It will make everyone's life a little easier.

19

Disabled

Legendary operators have always offered the same level of excellent service to all their guests. Disabled diners are people, too. They have some extra challenges in their lives and are among the most courageous people on the planet. All they ask is the same respect and opportunities for life that able-bodied people enjoy. Since dining out is one of life's pleasures, making the restaurant experience part of their lives is a special service you can provide. If you give them the service they want, they can be extremely loyal and enthusiastic guests. Your other diners will notice the compassion with which you treat the disabled and think of you more favorably.

Wheelchair on the premises   Not all disabled diners are permanently incapacitated. You will regularly have guests who are temporarily on crutches or older diners who have a difficult time navigating. Schneithorst's in St. Louis has a wheelchair in the coat room as a convenience for diners who are having a hard time moving about.

Seating close to the door   Disabled guests want to live their lives as normally as any of us. If the guest has some trouble navigating, it may be difficult for them to walk to a remote seat in the dining room. It also draws attention to them, something anyone would find uncomfortable. Seats by the door, which some diners find less desirable, are often ideal for disabled diners.

Braille menus   If a guest spoke another language, you would try to get someone who could translate, wouldn't you? Why not extend the same courtesy to deaf or blind guests? Most towns have a local agency that provides services for the blind. Ask them to translate your menu to Braille.

Menus on tape   A blind friend told me that only about 10% of blind people can read Braille. A seminar attendee had a wonderful idea—she had her entire menu recorded on a walkman-type recorder and offered it to blind diners. This way they could go through the menu at their own pace and still get the descriptions of the menu items.

Staff member who can sign   If you have someone on your staff who can speak sign language, you will open an entire new dining experience for deaf guests. There are many people who have learned to sign to communicate with hearing-impaired friends or family. Ask your staff if anyone has this skill.

TDD/TTY telephone   This device is essentially a teletype machine that will allow hearing-impaired guests to communicate with anyone. Talk with your local agencies for the deaf about how to get one installed in your restaurant.

Pad and pencil for deaf guests   If you are having a difficult time communicating with a deaf guest, simply provide a pad and pencil and use the written word to communicate.

Asking blind patrons if they want you to describe the location of the food   This is a small courtesy but one that can be appreciated by a blind patron dining alone. If they would like you to, tell them where things are in reference to a clock face. "The chicken is at 6:00, the potatoes are at 10:00" and so forth.

"Would you like the chef to cut the meat?"   This is a polite way to let a blind diner off the hook when they order an item, such as steak, that will need to be cut. It also does not assume that blind diners are incapable of fending for themselves in this area and gives them the option of taking you up on the offer or not.

20

Elderly

Socially and personally, dining is as much part of a satisfying life for seniors as for any of your other guests. Older diners grew up when standards of service were higher than those typically found today and they expect more. They know what they want and they know when they do (and don't) get it. Your ability to exceed the expectations of senior diners is a good measure of your professional skill.

Manager contact   Older people always like to know who is in charge and love attention from "the boss." They favor restaurants where the owner or manager actively works the floor.

Escort to the car   Seniors, especially women, have concern for their personal safety. They appreciate an escort to their cars in the evening. If you choose to provide this service, give seniors official notice of your offer. They are suspicious of strangers who offer to help. If possible, have your escorts wear your restaurant's uniform. It will help put elderly guests at ease.

Benefit of the doubt stance   A wonderful woman in her seventies told me of going to a restaurant near her home for lunch. When the check arrived, she realized she had left her wallet at home. She told the manager of her plight and was delighted when he trusted her to come back later to settle the bill. The point is that you can usually trust seniors. Give them the benefit of the doubt and you can make a friend for life.

Take-home menu   Many seniors do not cook, but still like to eat at home. Going to the market is often inconvenient for elderly people, so they appreciate the ability to get restaurant meals to go. An extensive menu of items available for take-home service can be very attractive to seniors. If you really want to serve the older market, consider a delivery service.

Prompt resolution of complaints   Never negotiate a guest's complaint. The only approach that will work is to apologize for the situation and fix it immediately. Do not ask the guest what they want you to do—it puts the guest on the spot and makes them uncomfortable. When you understand the nature and source of the problem, propose a generous solution that will make the guest happy. Remember that you are not just solving a problem, you are making an investment in securing a regular patron.

Location within walking distance   Many elderly people do not drive and prefer to patronize restaurants within walking distance of their home. You cannot move your business, but you *can* actively market your operation to seniors living in the neighborhood.

Single-priced buffet   Because of their fixed incomes, seniors like to know what their meal is going to cost. If your operation lends itself to this format, offering a fixed-price buffet will make you very popular with older diners. Make the fixed-price meal available during your slower hours when you have excess capacity. Since seniors eat less and go out as much for the social contact as for the meal, you are not taking much of a risk.

Armchairs   As people get older, their bodies become more fragile. Moving about becomes more difficult and simple tasks like sitting down and standing up take more work. Armchairs permit older diners to use their arms to get in and out of the chairs, making the process much easier. If all your chairs have arms, you are already elder-friendly. If not all your chairs have arms, moving the armchairs to the table before the older party is seated (and letting them know that you did it just for them) is delightful!

Respectful service   Unfortunately, our society often ignores senior citizens. This creates the opportunity for your restaurant to give seniors the recognition and respect denied to them elsewhere. While they have some special needs, older diners want the same enjoyable dining experience as any other guest in your restaurant. If you are compassionate enough to serve seniors with courtesy and respect, they will be your most loyal guests.

Give Guests Something Good to Talk About

21

Understanding Word of Mouth

Everybody says that [positive] word of mouth (WOM) is the best advertising, and I suspect that is true. But is it just a lucky accident or might there be more to it?

In my experience, the answer is definitely the latter because nothing happens by accident. Guests cannot talk about you unless they think about you . . . and think about you in the right way.

Creating these conditions in the minds of your guests is the result of a carefully crafted internal marketing program that you can create and control. This can potentially bring you more business than all the money you spend on more conventional advertising and at virtually no cost.

Does this sound too easy or too simple to be possible? Let me illustrate what the application of this principle did for me.

A Case Study

When I opened my first restaurant in the mid-1970s, a casual, full-service operation of my size in the financial district of San Francisco could expect a sales volume of around $600,000 a year. (Remember that this was at a time when well drinks were $1 and burgers sold for 3 bucks!) We did over $978,000 our first year and everyone was amazed. More than one competitor commented, "I don't understand it. Everyone in town is talking about your restaurant!" . . . and they were!

It was not an accident—we consciously set it up to be that way. We did no paid advertising other than a monthly one-inch insert in *San Francisco* magazine that consisted of our logo, address, and phone. We built our volume entirely on word of mouth. Our WOM success was the result of a conscious marketing program based on principles which I will explain in the pages that follow.

At the outset I must say that I can't promise that you will do 60% more volume than your competitors or even that you can garner an extra $378,000. There were a variety of factors at work in our achieving that sales volume. However, I can guarantee that the effective application of some simple ideas will help you tap this powerful medium for yourself.

Let's start by looking at the underlying principles of the WOM process and then discuss how you might apply these notions in your operation.

22

Basic Principles of WOM

This section of the book discusses a number of specific things you can do that will give guests many good things to talk about. It will help you to understand the underlying principles of the WOM process and how they serve and support the process of GBM.

The first principle that drives WOM is simply that

People cannot patronize you if they do not think of you!

The purpose of establishing a WOM program as it relates to GBM is as a way to get patrons talking positively about you. When you are part of an enthusiastic patron's conversation, the patron (and the people she talks to) will be reminded of you and therefore be motivated to return. Every time a guest thinks of you increases your potential for the repeat visit. It is safe to say that if your restaurant never enters her mind, she will never dine with you!

The second principle of WOM, and it is a big one, is that

There is no word of mouth without something to talk about.

If you want people to say wonderful things about you—and I am assuming that you do—they must have something to talk about. In other words, *you have to educate guests as to why they come to you.*

The third driving principle behind the WOM process is that

Word of mouth will not happen on its own.

While it is possible to have people say wonderful things about you without any work on your part, WOM is such a potent sales-building tool that you dare not leave it to chance. If you want people to talk, you have to take responsibility to make sure you give them plenty of good things to talk about. You have to get them more personally involved with your restaurant, earn their trust, tell them things they didn't know, and do things that are worth sharing with their families and friends.

The fourth principle of a WOM program is that:

Word of mouth depends on creating points of difference.

If you cannot create differences between yourself and your competitors, people will still be able to talk about you but they will not have as ready an answer to the question of "Why do you go to (your restaurant) so often?" People need reasons for what they do, so creating points of difference is another important aspect of GBM.

A final argument for an active WOM program as it relates to GBM is that *if you cannot create points of difference, you must compete strictly on the basis of price.*

Do you want to compete on price? If you could not make a case for the value difference between a Mercedes Benz and a Geo Metro, why would you pay $60,000 for a car?

The concept of creating points of difference is important in food-service.

A Burger Is a Burger . . . or Is It?

When discussing this point in my seminars, I typically ask who in the audience has a hamburger on the menu and what they charge for it. Most operators have a burger and the prices in a group have ranged from a low of $2.25 to nearly $7. Then I ask the person with the $7-burger why I should spend three times as much for his product. As a consumer, if I cannot clearly see the difference, or if that difference has no real value to me, there is no reason to pay a premium. If he *can* make the case, and if the differences are clear to me, the $7-burger may prove to be a better deal than the $2-product.

So what can we give people to talk about? In the pages that follow, I will present a few ideas to get your wheels turning. The list is not intended to cover all possibilities. If it did, this book would be presented in a three-volume set (if it could ever be finished at all)! Rather, the purpose is to suggest some possibilities that illustrate what can be done. The book leaves it to you to look at your own operation and determine what suggestions are most applicable.

One thing is for sure, people are going to talk about *something*. The only question is whether you want them to be talking about you or what they heard on the evening news. Since foodservice is a business based on personal interaction, let's start by looking at the human factors that figure into the success of a WOM program.

23

Why Do People Talk?

Everybody wants to have something to say and most people are not very original. I do not mean that as an indictment—it is just human nature.

Have you ever heard something—perhaps on the radio or TV or from a friend—and repeated it almost word-for-word to someone else? Did you know whether the information was 100% accurate or even question its correctness? My guess is that if the information was presented with certainty by a source you trusted, you took it at face value and passed it on to someone who had not heard it yet.

Moreover, I suspect you probably felt pretty good about having the information before they did and about being able to tell them something they did not know.

The Power of Inside Information

Everyone loves to know something that other people don't know. When they can pass along something to a friend that the friend did not know, it makes the passer look and feel more important, more connected to "what's happening." In addition, being first with the news can also enhance the passer's position with others. It may be an ego thing, but letting them in on a secret that they can share is a nice gift to give to your guests.

What secrets can you let people in on? It can be as simple as "leaking" the word that you have a wine special coming up before you announce it to the public. Tell them that you just located the last remaining case of 1978 Santa Cruz Pinot Noir on the planet and that you will not be putting it on the wine list but rather keeping it aside for those few insiders who know to ask for it.

Tell them about the things that fall into the "it's not on the menu but if you ask we will make it just for you" category. Sharing "secrets" is a great way to tie people more closely to your restaurant and to give them things to talk about!

Personal Involvement

People talk when they get involved with your products. If you have the best pot roast in town, you can create a loyal following from pot roast fanatics, particularly if they know how it is prepared, why you selected the cut of meat you use, where your recipe came from, why your pot roast is better or different and so forth.

People also talk when they get involved with themselves. This can happen when you help your guests feel like pioneers by trying something new or unusual.

For example, when I was catering international functions for the Olympic Committee, one of my favorite items to include on a reception menu was rattlesnake chili. This was not because there was some pent-up demand for rattlesnake (I assure you there was not!) but because guests would talk about it, often for a year or more, whether they tried it or not!

That same process can be profitably applied in your restaurant (hotel/club/bowling center/resort/bank/whatever).

In the pages that follow, I will share a few ideas on what you can do to get people talking about you and how you can be sure they will say what you want them to say!

24

Who Do People Listen To?

In general, people are suspicious of commercials. People censor information that comes in on the commercial channel pretty heavily because there is an obvious motive to the message— somebody wants to sell you something. I always like to *buy*, but I rarely like to *be sold*.

People listen to people they know and like. They do not seem to have the same skepticism for information that they hear from friends as they do for information they receive from strangers, particularly strangers with a motive.

This is why some companies use celebrity endorsers to push their products. The premise of the celebrity endorser is that if you trust the endorser, you will tend to trust that he would not steer you wrong about a product or service he endorses. You know that he is getting paid obscene amounts of money to lend his name to the product and that he may not have any demonstrated knowledge in the area he is endorsing, but that does not seem to be a major disadvantage. The goal is to give the product credibility by association and it works.

I doubt that you can afford celebrity endorsers for your restaurant (although you might have some well-known people in your regular clientele) but you do not need the big names. You have access to a source of endorsement that is even more trusted than celebrities: your everyday patrons who talk to their friends and family . . . every day.

People listen to people they trust. Information that arrives on the "friends and family" channel is not resisted because there is no motive behind the message. People are more likely to listen to family, friends, and neighbors who have nothing to gain from an endorsement. Information from these sources is usually accepted without skepticism.

People will also listen to knowledgeable people—recognized authorities in a particular area of expertise—but only as long as there is no direct motive.

For example, if your chef makes an appearance on a TV show, they will trust her opinion as a chef with regard to the best way to roast a turkey. But as soon as she starts talking about what a great restaurant you have and asking people to make reservations for Thanksgiving dinner, she once again becomes a commercial source and her words will be greeted with more suspicion.

My suggestion is that you will not build (much) word of mouth for your restaurant by giving commercial-like pitches.

The route to higher repeat patronage and higher sales volume using word of mouth comes from acting as a recognized authority about your products and services without an obvious sales motive. In this role, you can more easily educate your guests about what you are doing that is better or different so that they can carry the message to others on the (uncensored) friends and family network.

25

A Few Thoughts about People

This is only an observation, but I believe most people are relatively unsure of themselves.

To counter this insecurity, or perhaps just because our minds seem to work this way, people seem to need reasons to justify their decisions ("The reason I do this is because . . ."). Think about it. If someone asked why you drive the particular car you do, your response would likely begin, "I drive a _____ because . . ." You are not likely to say, "Gee, I never thought about it!"

If you want guests to patronize your operation more often—and remember that the safe route to the big bucks is just to get current guests back just one additional time each month—then they need reasons to justify their increased patronage. In other words, you have to educate your guests so that they will know why they dine with you. The rationale is still "I go there because . . ."

The mission, if you want to profit from this tendency, is to fill in the blank for your guests—to be sure they know why they come to you so they will have the justification they need to continue to do it!

26

Goals of a WOM Program

A successful word of mouth program has five principal goals:

1. Educate your patrons

It is important that people know why they come to you. When you can do that, you give people reasons for dining with you. The more they know about what you are doing for them and what makes it better or different, the easier it will be for them to complete the statement, "I go there because _____."

2. Make a salesperson out of the guest

The more your guests know about what you are doing for them the more they will have to talk about, particularly if you make them privy to information that not everyone else knows. If you want your guests to go out and talk to others about you (and you do!) you have to make sure they have something to tell their friends.

3. Give guests reasons to come back

Remember that the key to building volume is repeat patronage. You will make far more money by getting a guest back one more time a month than you will by trying to pry every dollar you can from their clutching fingers tonight. In order for them to come back, they need a reason, and it falls to you to give them one or more reasons to return.

4. Make the service more personal

In addition to giving people something to talk about, when you are actively educating your guests about why they come to your restaurant, it helps make the service more personal. Through consistent coaching, the service staff will always be aware of natural opportunities to educate guests and this will give them something more productive and personal to say at the table than "how's everything?"

5. Differentiate the operation

People cannot come to you if they do not think of you. The more you can differentiate yourself from other operations, the less you will be forced to compete on the basis of price and the more reasons people will have to think of you when they go elsewhere. You want them to see you in an entirely different light than they regard all other restaurants.

27

Differentiate the Basics

While it is definitely to your advantage to create elements and products that are unique to your operation, it is also important to create points of difference in those items you know that every other restaurant offers. If you are successful in doing this, you will give guests reasons to think of you every time they dine elsewhere.

So what does every other restaurant offer? Let's start with the basics—items like water, napkins, coffee, soft drinks, beer, wine, salad, bread, restrooms, and telephones.

In general, you can create a point of difference in any of these items either in the product itself, in the way it is presented, or in any policies you might have with regard to it. Here are some ideas to get you started thinking how you might be able to exploit these differences to your advantage:

	Product	Presentation/Policy
Water	local spring water imported water bottled water (esp. if no extra charge) specially filtered water	pressed glass bottle carafe service flower petal in the glass
Napkins	oversized different material (calico, towel)	napkin rings hot towels before/after the meal
Coffee	special blend flavored coffees espresso and cappuccino	oversized or crested mugs carafe service brewed at the table
Soft drinks	bottled vs. post mix extensive selection	free refills carafe service
Beer	extensive microbrew menu extensive imported beer list local/regional brews	unusual glassware personalized mugs bottles served in a bucket of ice

Wine	little-known vineyards	oversized wine glasses
	extensive wine list	higher quality glassware
	moderate pricing policy	for upper end wines
		pouring house wine at
		the table
Salad	unusual ingredients	unusual salad bowls
	exceptionally chilled	oversized salad bowls
	house-made dressings	
Bread	exceptional, piping	served on an individual
	hot bread	cutting board
	drop biscuits	served on sheet pans hot
	quick breads	from the oven
Restrooms	dual restrooms (2 for	amenities
	men, 2 for women	panic button
	vs. 1 of each)	ice in the urinals
	over-fixturing and extra	
	space	
Telephones	sound effects panel	notepads by the phone
	foreign phone booth	free local phone calls
	unusual privacy or comfort	tableside phones

Any good thing can be overdone. It probably goes without saying, but as you start to add elements to differentiate your operation, keep the bigger picture in mind. Any of these distinctions can help set one operation apart from another, but not all of them are appropriate for every restaurant and trying to implement *all* of them is inappropriate for *anyone.*

28

What Can You Talk About?

If you want people to talk about you, to spread the good word, to become a salesperson for your restaurant, guests must have something specific to tell their friends.

For example, it is not enough that guests simply have a good time when they come in. If that is all that happens, all they can tell other people is that they had a good time. That is better than nothing, but it doesn't have much "talking power." On the other hand, if you make sure they know *why* they had a good time, then they have a story to tell.

With a little guest education, they could say something like this:

> "We were at Monty's last night and really had a great time! Did you know that they have their own garden in the back? They made us this great salad and the lettuce had just been picked that afternoon. You wouldn't believe what an incredible taste it had—easily the best salad I ever ate! I tell you, the next time a restaurant goes on and on about freshness and then serves me week-old iceberg lettuce, I'm heading for the door!"

Do you see the "talking power" in this scenario and how simple it would be to educate guests on these points (we have our own garden, the greens were picked this afternoon, anyone who serves week-old iceberg lettuce can't be very serious about freshness) at some time during the meal?

Do you think these people—and their friends—are more likely to go back to Monty's? When they go to one of Monty's competitors and get the predictable iceberg lettuce, would you guess that they will think of Monty? It's the old "I could have had a V-8" idea.

Of course, it helps if you do things that are worth talking about in the first place, but it is equally important to make sure people know what you have done for them, whatever it happens to be.

29

Concept

O ne of the first places to look for differentiation is in the concept of the restaurant itself. Your concept is the operating premise of the place—the way you want people to think of you. With many markets reaching saturation and with new restaurants opening every day, it is impractical to think that "if you build it they will come."

People need reasons for what they do, and the way you put your concept together can be a major factor in why people will try you out in the first place and talk to their friends (favorably) about you after they leave. Here are a few ideas.

Cuisine   Being the first restaurant in the area to offer a particular cuisine will set you apart from every other competitor who comes after you. For example, if you are the first barbecue joint in Topeka, no one else can ever claim to be the oldest rib house in Topeka nor could they use the title of Topeka's original barbecue. Use this distinction to your advantage.

Combination of cuisines   At this stage in the development of most restaurant market areas, the principal cuisines are probably already represented. Even so, there may still be a way to differentiate yourself based on the type of food you offer.

As an example, let me present a case study based on a past project—a Colorado restaurant that had been a rib house for about 12 years. It was badly in need of renovation and while sales once exceeded $1 million a year, over the prior 6 years, volume had slipped by over 50%. The trend was not exciting and the owner knew he had to do something. At the same time, he was reasonably sure that just fresh paint and new carpeting would not be enough to make it a high-grossing operation. He retained me to study the situation and see what could be done to revitalize the business.

To become a high-volume operation, I felt that the restaurant would have to be at the forefront of people's minds: they had to want to go there. It could not be just one more dining option. I did not want to have to slug it out for market share with another operator in order to succeed, at least not if there was any way to avoid it.

Now, it was a moderately credible rib operation and people obviously looked at it as a place for barbecue. However, it did not have the reputation as the premier rib joint in the market. Another restaurant had become known in the local market as the place to go for ribs and that "top-of-mind" position made them formidable, even if their product was not as good.

My first thought was to update the concept and make it more distinctive. I considered changing the name to "The Big Pig," having some outrageous t-shirts printed, and doing some unusual things in the way of decor and service to make the dining experience more fun. Changes like this would help but they were unlikely to ever make us the first place people thought of when they wanted ribs.

The building had some tile on the roof and had a certain southwestern feeling, so a Mexican-style restaurant would fit architecturally. Mexican food was popular in town but there had been Mexican restaurants in the area for 40 years, so we were not likely to ever be the pre-eminent Mexican operation either.

Then it occurred to me that while barbecue and Mexican were both popular dining choices, nobody in town offered *both* barbecue and Mexican on the same menu. The two cuisines were compatible (I would not have been as quick to combine Chinese and Italian!) and we proceeded to develop a food concept called border barbecue. Because we would be the first to put these two together, we could effectively create a new food category where we would be first in the minds of the market.

Differentiation Is Important

Le Central in Denver bills itself as "the affordable French restaurant," and Macheezmo Mouse is pushing "healthy Mexican food." What twists can you give your place to be more memorable?

Name

Clever names can give people something to talk about provided the name has some staying power and the restaurant has more going for it than just the name.

David Duthie owns a delightful restaurant in Lambertville, New Jersey called The Yellow Brick Toad! He says the name sounded better to him when he opened in 1978 than it does today, but he has such a reputation and a loyal following that he doesn't dare tinker with it. Still, the name was unusual enough to get people talking about him when he first opened and at least give him a try. The rest was up to him.

We played the name game in the Colorado project as well. The market where our prototype border barbecue was located was, well, boring. Most of the restaurants were locally owned independents—serviceable but not very imaginative. I felt that this created an opportunity to make an impact with an unusual name. The name we came up with was El Puerco Border BBQ, Cosmetic Surgery and Small Engine Repair!

It was a little over the edge, but we figured people would remember the name and talk about it. Our premise was that diners would have to come in at least once just to see what in the world we were up to . . . and if we could get them in once, we could get them back. We could also shorten the name to simply El Puerco Border BBQ sometime in the future when we were more firmly established and if the novelty of the name had worn off.

Method of Service

The first drive-in restaurant in town was something everyone had to experience. In many parts of the country, the old cafeteria concept has been reinvented as the buffet. Exhibition kitchens are the latest design element and who knows what else is possible. One of these days I will do an all-you-can-eat restaurant with trough service and see what sort of reaction it gets!

Market Niche

How are you perceived in the minds of the market? The marketing battle is fought between the ears, and how people think of you determines what you are to them. For example, many people delivered pizza before Domino's arrived on the scene. But Domino's was the first pizza company to declare that "delivery are us." In doing so, they claimed the pizza delivery position in the minds of the market.

If nobody in town is known as the place for families, you could lay claim to it. Could you become *the* place to go for special occasions? How about the most fun or the most casual place to eat? Is anyone regarded as the most healthy dining choice? Are you the oldest or the most historic restaurant in the market?

I did some work years ago with a lovely Italian restaurant, The Villa in Palmer Lake, located about 20 miles from the center of Colorado Springs. The food was superb, the atmosphere intimate, and the service impeccable. As good as they were, they did not have more business than they could handle, except perhaps on some weekends. My suggestion was that they declare that "The Villa is for lovers" and become known as the place to go for a romantic dinner with someone you really care about. People could get Italian food without driving 20 miles, but if the Villa was for lovers, it was in another category.

This market position could be reinforced with menu items designed to be shared, a selection of wines in the half bottle, and perhaps even price fixe dinners for two. It would definitely sidestep the issue of which Italian restaurant has the best (cheapest/most authentic) veal piccata!

The point here is for you to determine how you want to be regarded in the market (or what categories are unclaimed in people's minds), claim it for your own, and reinforce it at the table and in your advertising. For a more detailed discussion of how this process works, I suggest *Bottom Up Marketing* by Trout and Ries (see "Resources" on page 203).

30

Operating Policies

How you choose to operate your business is a fertile ground for WOM. Here are a few policies that might have "talking power" for you.

Smoking Policies

If you are the first full-service restaurant in your market to go entirely nonsmoking, that is a point of difference that you (and your guests) can talk about. The percentage of the population who smoke is declining, there is more in the media about the dangers of second-hand smoke, and antismoking legislation is becoming more and more common. If you wait until a state law or local ordinance bans smoking in all restaurants, you will have nothing to discuss—if you move first, you will.

This can be a positive policy for operators whose physical plants make it difficult to keep smoke from drifting into nonsmoking areas. Small restaurants in particular might find this the only truly workable option for them.

Making the change to a smoke-free facility can work when your market is largely families. When the Dunes Restaurant in Nags Head, North Carolina decided to eliminate smoking, they expected some resistance. It is true that North Carolina grows a lot of tobacco(!) and a few guests took offense at the policy. They were mollified with the explanation that "We did it for the babies." The staff explained that they had so many families as guests and they were just uncomfortable about exposing children to second-hand smoke. Most people understood and stayed to eat.

The decision to eliminate smoking is not the right move for everyone as it will definitely inconvenience a portion of your market, particularly in operations with a significant bar business. If your restaurant lends itself to total separation of smokers from nonsmokers, there is no particular reason to change. However, if you allow smoking while your competitors are going smoke-free, you can create a point of difference with your smoking patrons by reminding them that they are not treated like second-class citizens when they dine with you.

There are several well-funded and well-supported programs to encourage the peaceful co-existence of smokers and nonsmokers. They can provide you with window decals, table tents, and training aids to help you and your staff do a better job of making everyone feel welcome. For more information, see the "Resources" chapter on page 203.

Even restaurants that are otherwise smoke-free are finding that monthly cigar dinners are tremendously popular (and profitable!). It is interesting that as cigarette smoking is falling out of favor, the cigar industry is experiencing a boom!

Service Guarantee

Service guarantees are the natural result of a guest-oriented business posture. When you offer an unconditional service guarantee, you pledge to do whatever is necessary to assure your guests have a wonderful experience in your restaurant. It is going to cost you some money to carry out an effective service guarantee, but the idea may not be as radical as it sounds.

If your guests have a problem, you will make it right for them, won't you? If so, you already have a toe in the water of service guarantees. All this policy suggests is that you become proactive rather than reactive—that you obligate yourself before the fact to do what you are already willing to do after the fact.

I know, I know. You figure that people will take advantage of you if you do this, and you are right. There are some who will, but not the swarm you fear. Hampton Inns has a 100% satisfaction guarantee—just say that you didn't like the room and there is no charge. You would think that people would really take advantage of a chance to stay for free, but my source at the company tells me that it is about 3/10 of 1%—3 in 1,000 actually take them up on it!

Would you sell at a 0.3 discount? No-brainer question, right? Why would you balk at a service guarantee? We tend to make the rules for the 3 complainers and forget the 997 who will be thrilled that we are so committed to their well-being. Besides, if your guests are not having a good time, it is already costing you money. You just don't know how much. Paying off on the guarantee will quickly point out the breakdowns in your system so you can correct them.

If people go to your restaurant and don't enjoy themselves, they are going have a bad memory of the experience, never return, and say terrible things about you to their friends. In other words, if you blow it, you are going to take the hit anyway, so what have you got to lose by taking responsibility? Besides, if a guest knows he can come to you and be guaranteed a great time or go to your competitors and take his chances, what do you think he will do?

The key to an effective service guarantee is to look for opportunities to correct situations before the guest even realizes that he has a problem. You cannot wait for people to tell you because only one in 24 will actually do it. The rest go away and most of them don't come back, service guarantee or not.

For example, a friend of mine had a restaurant in Portland, Oregon. One of his standards was a 15-minute ticket time. Going through the dining room one night, he noticed a table that did not have their entrees and it seemed to him that it had been longer than 15 minutes since they had placed their orders. He checked it out and it was close to 20 minutes. He went into the kitchen and brought the order out himself.

As he placed the meal on the table, he said, "Gentlemen, I am so sorry. This took far longer than our norm, so first of all I want you to know that your dinners are on me tonight. Second, I would like you to accept these gift certificates to come back as my guests because I would like to show you that we can do a better job than this."

The guests were astounded. "Great," they said, "but we really didn't notice." He responded, "Maybe you didn't notice, but *we* did!" That is a service guarantee!

Free Beverages If You Have to Wait

I remember when the first Pacific Cafe opened in San Francisco in the mid-1970s. It was out toward the beach in a predominantly residential area. The location was not particularly prime and the weather was often cold and foggy. It was a small restaurant and had no place inside for guests to wait.

One night shortly after they opened, the manager saw a waiting line extending down the sidewalk. Feeling sorry that his guests had to wait in the cold, he offered free wine to everyone until they could be seated. Needless to say, the waiting patrons loved it and didn't mind the wait anymore.

The word spread quickly because it was a great story and every-one who heard the story passed it along. I heard about it within a day or two. Curious to see what they were doing, a group of friends and I went over for dinner. There was a line down the sidewalk and they were out there pouring the wine. I have a vague memory that we had dinner that night (it was quite a wait) but we hung in there! Our wait was far longer that we ever would have accepted any-where else, but none of us minded because we were being so well cared for!

The practice became a tradition. The waiting line (and the com-plimentary wine) continues to this day. I am sure that somewhere there is an accountant going crazy! The restaurant has had a line out the door since 1976. I don't think it bothers them!

I told that story at the Virginia Restaurant Show several years ago and heard from the operator who tried it. He had a restaurant on the strip in South Richmond along with all the other national mid-scale chains. That year, Valentine's Day fell on a Friday so he knew it would be a particularly busy night and that many people would not make reservations. He remembered the wine story and decided he had nothing to lose, so he invested in two cases of cheap champagne. Whenever he was on a wait, he would advise the couple that it would be a few minutes but that the champagne was on him until he could seat them. He says he did at least $4,000 in business that would otherwise have walked . . . and it cost him $60 to do it!

By the way, free champagne is great because so many people will have one glass then go back to their regular drink at full price! When I was crafting the El Puerco project in Colorado, we were in a market where people would not wait at all. My policy was that if you had to wait, your drinks were free until we could seat you. If you wanted to drink Jack Daniels, that was fine with me. I figured people would say, "Let's go there. We might have to wait!"

I talk a lot about free alcohol, but the power behind this idea isn't the offer of spirits as much as the spirit behind the offer. Your operation (or your state laws) may not make it practical to offer free alcohol, but how about offering coffee or soft drinks to waiting guests? You could pass a tray of complimentary hors d'oeuvres among waiting guests.

As a final note, if you implement a policy like this, don't advertise it, just do it. It will make the offer more personal and keep it as a "secret" for diners to tell their friends.

Pricing

The way you price your menu can provide food for talk. If you offer an all-you-can-eat policy where your competitors don't, that is a point of difference you can exploit. Steve Miller, a leading industry educator, has a suggestion along this line: To get more talking power from an all-you-can-eat policy, call it instead "enough." So your menu now says "enough shrimp." When guests ask how much is enough, you can say that it is up to them to decide! The policy is the same but there is more to talk about.

Another variation on this idea is to offer free second helpings. It can really take diners by surprise when the server asks them if they would like more _____. You can explain that this is a policy you implement to be sure that guests always have as much as they want to eat and that this way their food will always be hot. (It also helps assure that you minimize plate waste which in itself might generate enough savings to fund any additional costs involved.)

A point of difference for a steakhouse is to price the meat by the ounce, a policy pioneered by Phil Lehr in San Francisco. Guests select their cut of meat at a counter and specify how thick they want it cut. Whether they want 5 ounces or 25 ounces, they can get it. This policy creates a point of difference in the meat, gets the guest more involved with the restaurant, and eliminates losses from under- or over-portioning.

If you offer a lower price than your competitors, you can be sure guests know it. If you have the highest prices in town, you can educate guests as to why you are worth the premium. Loss leaders, combos and fixed-price menus, are other examples of differences based on a pricing policy.

History of the Restaurant

If your restaurant has a story, you must tell it. You can't count on menu copy to do that for you because most people do not *read* menus, they *scan* menus. The effectiveness of menu copy is further reduced by the tendency of servers to snatch the menus back at the first opportunity! If you want people to talk, you have to give them the words, a process that we will examine in more detail in Chapter 36.

The story of your restaurant can include a variety of factors, both historical and personal. Let me suggest a few to get you thinking.

If you are located in an old building, what is the history of the building itself? When was it built and what has it been used for over the years? How did the various activities once conducted in the building figure into the history of the area? Who were the past owners of the building and what was their role in the development of the area? Do you have pieces of decor, furniture, or fixtures with an interesting story? If the name of the restaurant has a story, where did it come from and why did you select it? If the building is new, what stood on the site in the past?

What are the backgrounds of the restaurant owners? Is there one of those rags-to-riches stories of immigrant grandparents starting with eight stools in a converted garage and building it into a multi-unit chain? If so, tell it, preferably with a few poignant pictures. If the owners are new to the restaurant business (the job of owner *is* one of the entry-level positions in our industry!), what were they doing before opening the restaurant? Why did they decide to get into the restaurant business? What is their business philosophy? Think in terms of "sound bites" not a manifesto, please!

Weaknesses/Lapses in the Competition

You should never bad-mouth the competition, but it is definitely to your advantage for your guests to know why you are better or different from other restaurants in the market. The most potent points of difference are the ones that address those areas where your competitors are weakest or least likely to change.

You see it in chain competition all the time. Because McDonald's cooks their hamburgers on a grill, Burger King can make a point of difference on the fact that they flame-broil their burgers. Is McDonald's going to re-tool their restaurants? Not likely. Even if the difference in cooking method proved to be wildly popular with the market and Burger King was taking market share, McDonald's would be hard-pressed to change. If they did, it would only give more credibility to the Burger King claims and make McDonald's into a "me too" company.

A similar process can work when you are competing with a chain restaurant. Chains achieved their position by virtue of a defined concept and a set format. There are strengths in that, of course, but the weakness is that they are unable to make many changes in what they do. Even if they can change, it will be a slow process.

An independent operator can compete successfully with the chains simply by taking advantage of their relative rigidity. Greg Hunsucker is a co-owner of V's, an old-line Italian restaurant in Kansas City. Several years ago, Olive Garden opened about a half mile away and immediately drained a significant sales volume from V's. They expected their guests would check out the newcomers at least once so when guests came in, he would ask if they had visited the new chain. When they got the report, they would say, "Well, there's more to Italian food than just salad and bread sticks!" The next time these guests returned to Olive Garden, they noticed . . . and thought of V's. They regained their lost volume (and more) by exploiting one of Olive Garden's signature points— one that they were not likely to ever change!

If you think about it, you can always identify weaknesses or lapses in other restaurants. Do they have a ventilation problem? Do they not have a view like yours? Will their concept make it impossible for them to offer a particular item? Do they not serve hot food hot? Is their staff robot-like? Do they make you wait forever? Is their parking a problem? Are their prices higher or their portions smaller? Almost any detail can be turned to your advantage if you are aware of what others are doing, if you can find a way to do something clearly better or different (and if you are willing to tell your guests about it!).

31

Food and Beverage

People do come to restaurants to eat and drink, so it is important to educate guests about differences in our food and beverage products.

Product knowledge   This is basic but it is too often overlooked. Most restaurants do only a fair job of educating their servers about what is on the menu, and the servers do not even attempt to educate the guests. Product knowledge is more than just memorizing what you have on the menu. It includes knowing what makes each product better or different and the ability to communicate those differences clearly to the guests.

Signature items   Remember that people need reasons for what they do ("I go there because . . ."). So what are you famous for? What do I absolutely have to try when I come to your restaurant? What item do you do better than anyone else in town? What can I get in your restaurant that I cannot get anywhere else?

If you are not famous for something, *declare* yourself famous for something! Certainly you should have a signature entree but how about a signature appetizer, a signature salad, and a signature dessert? Have you developed a signature bread? Do you have a signature before-dinner drink, a signature after-dinner drink, and a signature coffee? If not, why not?

How about a signature side dish? Tadich Grill, the oldest restaurant in San Francisco, is as known among the locals for its creamed spinach as for its fresh fish. Somebody in town will have a reputation for the best onion rings, the best fried zucchini, or the best hash browns. Why couldn't it be you?

Signatures do not even have to be an all-the-time thing—you can have seasonal signatures. Steve Miller suggests a "special winter slaw" that you only serve in January and February (when the quality of lettuce is in the basement and the price is through the roof).

Your staff and your guests will ultimately identify your best items. In fact, your signatures may turn out to be items other than the ones you thought they would be. Don't let that bother you. Once your signature items are identified, make sure they are noted as such on your menu. When a guest opens the menu, it should be clear what items you want them to order.

Source of your recipes   Are you using old family recipes? Did they come from a celebrity? Are they the product of someone on your staff? If there is a story behind your recipes, tell it.

Here is an example from my old San Francisco restaurant: One of my cooks, Al Drake, made incredible soup, so we did not have a "Soup of the Day"—our menu listed "Al's Soup." We did the same with desserts ("Joan's Cheesecake" sounds better and has more talking power than "New York Style Cheesecake"). We had "Paul's Special"—meatless entrees created by Paul Ross, our vegetarian cook. The guests liked it better and my staff was thrilled by the recognition.

Source of ingredients   There is a reason you have selected every ingredient that goes into your menu items. Do you ever talk to your guests about what you have done and why? If you use premium ingredients, you have to let your guests know about it. Did your beef come from a local ranch? Do you use organic produce? Is that Grey Poupon dijon mustard that you use in the dijonnaise sauce? All of these are things that people might talk about, but only if you tell them what you have done.

Cost of ingredients   Interestingly enough, people are fascinated by prices. Several years ago, I developed an adult fast food restaurant for a client featuring superb hot dogs and sausages. When someone would comment on the tastiness of the hot dogs (and most did), we might say, "You know, our wholesale price per pound on that hot dog is higher than the retail price of steak in the supermarket!" The statement was true and I am willing to bet that the guests who heard it were inclined to pass that statement along to their friends. I also expect they thought of our hot dogs every time they went to the store and saw the steak!

Presentation   There are several other factors that can put more "talking power" into your food and beverage presentations. How an item is garnished can be a factor. Do you think you could market a southwestern martini with a jalapeño pepper in it? How about fresh nasturtiums on the plate—they are edible and different.

You could offer an item with an unusual sauce. You could serve an item with three different sauces or offer a choice of sauces. Kentucky Fried Chicken would taste the same without the phrase "eleven secret herbs and spices," but the words have stuck and people talk about it. Could you develop a "secret blend of spices" to give a signature item more word of mouth potential?

Presentation could also be a special china or specialty glassware. Oversized wine glasses can be delightful. When a guest orders a bottle of his upper end wines, Randy Rayburn of Sunset Grill in Nashville brings out the crystal wine glasses. The range of colorful specialty plates and platters available today is extensive and can enhance even the most modest of dishes. Murray's in Minneapolis serves their signature "Silver Butter Knife Steak" for two on a plank and carves it at the table. Delightful!

Portion sizes   How much you put on the plate can be a talking point. If you have large portions, it is worth talking about. Smaller portions at smaller prices can be something different.

On the beverage side, you can serve wines by the glass or by the taste. You can even serve wine based on consumption—if you only drink half the bottle, you only get charged for half the bottle!

Preparation methods   Do you use any special equipment? If so, tell your guests about it so that they can tell their friends. Is it a particularly expensive piece of gear? Tell people how much it costs. They will be appropriately impressed and will pass it along. "And they have this incredible machine that makes the tortillas from the raw dough right in front of you! It costs over $25,000! You've got to see it!"

Have you come up with an improved variation on a traditional method of preparation?

Mike Nemeth owns a legendary Mexican restaurant in Colorado Springs. After noticing that his guests were becoming more nutritionally conscious, he decided to offer a chimichanga (usually a deep-fried burrito) that is crisped in the oven rather than in a fryer. It tastes as good or better than the fried version without the added fat. If he tells his guests what he is doing, they can pass the word to others. (If he does not tell his guests, he loses an opportunity.)

Wood roasting is an old way of cooking but relatively new to modern restaurant kitchens. If you cook over a wood fire, you can talk about it. Do you have a special rub that you put on the meat before cooking? Talk about it. Do you prepare to order when your competitors cook things ahead? Talk about it.

New products or out-of-fashion products revisited   People are fascinated by new or unusual products. They don't always order them but they will talk about them. I mentioned the rattlesnake chili I used to include on reception menus, but a new product could be something like vegetable pastas. Mike Hurst found Morton Bay bugs in Australia, crawfish-like critters that taste a lot like lobster. They started off as a novelty item on his menu—imagine going out to dinner and ordering bugs! They are now his most popular entree and one that everyone still talks about. What unusual or under-utilized species of fish can you work into *your* menu?

Some products are not new, just rediscovered. Sun-dried tomatoes have been around for centuries but are appearing on restaurant menus again. You might want to be on the lookout for new herbs or spices from other countries that can be incorporated into more traditional menu items. Sam Arnold, owner of The Fort in Morrison, Colorado has a special pepper (as in salt and pepper) that he imports from a small island in the South Pacific. He discovered it on one of his trips and it makes for a good story.

Menu presentation   Your menu can be something to talk about. It could be in the way it is presented to the guest. A verbal menu can work if it is small and accompanied by a written version. It could be in the physical nature of the menu itself. Menus on gold pans, bottles, paddles, or boards were once the rage and might make a comeback in themed operations. The menu at Fifteenth Street Fisheries in Ft. Lauderdale is a framed presentation set on an easel by the side of the table.

Range of items   You could make a point of difference based on the range of items you offer. For example, if you had a large menu, you could say, "The great thing about a big menu is that everyone can always find something they like." If you had a small menu, you could say, "We only have ten items on our menu because we think a restaurant can only do a credible job with a limited menu. If a place has a huge menu, you know that many of the items have to be filler." Who is right? It depends on whether you have a large menu or a small menu!

32

Decor

Restaurants are a visual experience as well as a culinary one. When people are not actually eating, they are looking around. What do they see and what can they say about it? Here are a few thoughts on using decor to stimulate word-of-mouth.

Valuable art pieces   Museum-quality art or sculpture is certainly something to talk about. Not every operation can afford to go too far in this direction, but even a single, memorable piece with a story can do wonders to get people talking.

Collections   Even if your budget does not run to original Picassos, collections can be fun. Lambert's Cafe in Missouri has a collection of mule pictures. The Thirsty Turtle restaurant in Bernardsville, New Jersey has (surprise!) a turtle collection. There are restaurants with vintage model trains running around the ceiling or original Tiffany stained glass pieces. In most cases, the collection reflects the interests of the owner or the theme of the restaurant, but in either case it is something for the guests to talk about. Often, diners will even bring in pieces to add to the collection.

Flower arrangements   Most people have no idea what can be done with flowers. Their experience with large floral displays is typically limited to what they see at weddings and funerals! If your restaurant lends itself to it, an elaborate floral display, properly lighted, can be worth talking about. At the least it is something that people do not see every day. The cost can be high, but have you priced display ads lately?

Unusual features   Any unexpected touches can generate conversation. A great view has always been in demand, but even man-made elements can work for you. An elaborate fountain, an indoor waterfall, an exquisite mural, a vine-covered patio, or an open deck can set you apart from competitors with less imagination.

Attractively coordinated tabletops   Take a few minutes to look at your tabletop objectively. Does it have impact? Would a guest look at the setting and be impressed? Your choice of flatware, glassware, table appointments, and china must all work together visually, be of the proper scale for the size of the table, and be appropriate to the look of the room and the check average of the meal. You will know if you are on the right track when you get a spontaneous, positive comment from the guests when they are shown to the table.

33

Design

A restaurant can be designed with features that give guests something to talk about. While a complete renovation may not be practical, here are a few ideas to consider when you are planning a remodeling or new construction.

Dual restrooms   When you design your next restaurant, consider putting in two sets of restrooms instead of just one. It will let you make each of the rooms a little smaller (and therefore a little less institutional-feeling), minimize the amount of walking the guests have to do, and give you some slack when a restroom is being cleaned or is out of service for some reason.

Exhibition cooking   If your operation lends itself to it, consider an exhibition kitchen next time. People love to watch their food being prepared and it provides some drama in the dining room. Some people are fascinated by what it takes to put out meals in a restaurant. Others are reassured to be able to see how their meals are being handled. But whatever the reason, exhibition kitchens are increasingly more common in new restaurant construction. If you want to see how to really do this right, go to the Contemporary Hotel at Walt Disney World in Orlando and check out the California Grill.

Counter space at the pay phone   Many people need to put down an address book or make notes when they are talking on the phone. A small counter will make the phones more guest-friendly. A supply of pencils and note paper (with the restaurant's logo, name, and address, of course) will be particularly delightful!

Canopy over the drive-up window   In inclement weather, who wants water dripping into their bag of burgers? A canopy protects your guests (and your products) from the weather and makes the drive-up experience more friendly.

Individual volume controls   When we renovated the dining room at the Olympic Training Center, we put two big screen television sets at the end of the room so they were easily visible from every table. Rather than trying to blast the sound to the far ends of the room, we wired the television speakers into the sound system. There were 13 different sets of speakers in the dining room, each set with its own volume control. The athletes could turn the volume up to hear the TV sound track or down if they did not want the interruption. We did not have to turn the television volume up to the threshold of pain to have it project to the back of the dining room. The athletes had more control over their dining environment, and the sound quality was much better.

Tableside phones   This is a particular attraction to salespeople who do most of their scheduling by phone. Some restaurants have free local telephones permanently mounted at many of their tables. Cordless telephones can be an easy solution when the dining room layout makes it impractical to install wired tableside phones. Several companies even offer cordless phones that link to a computer to provide a printout of charges for both local and long-distance calls.

If you provide tableside phones merely as a gimmick, their benefit will be short-lived. If they are an amenity that provides an unexpected service or convenience to guests in need, they will add to your reputation for guest service and give diners something to talk about.

Divided dining areas   Smaller dining areas create a sense of intimacy and comfort that most guests don't experience in a more open room. Low dividers, half walls, planters, plants, and level changes give the dining room visual interest and break up the space.

Individual light dimmers   Many people, but particularly older diners, need bright light to read the menu and prefer more subdued lighting during the meal. Some solo diners like to read or work while they enjoy their meal. Obviously one preset level of illumination will not be universally satisfactory. Particularly if your dining room has high-backed booths, consider wiring the table lighting through individual dimmers. This will allow each guest to have the lighting just the way they want it.

Private dining rooms   There are many reasons people go out that could be enhanced by privacy. Small business meetings, special occasion celebrations, or a romantic evening can become more enjoyable and unique in a private setting. Private dining rooms can open new markets for business. You can close them off when they are not needed to make the dining area appear comfortably full on slower nights, and you can open them into the main dining room for use during peak periods. Private dining rooms can be an effective way to make odd spaces more productive.

Professional design   When professionals have designed a restaurant's interior design, lighting, sound, and layout, the result can be breathtaking. In many markets, designers may have their own following. The fact that a certain designer "did" the restaurant is something to talk about.

Bringing this level of talent to bear on a project can be expensive, but if the restaurant can consistently deliver on its promises, the return can be worthwhile. Even if you do not employ a professional to do the complete design, you can pay a small consulting fee for some professional input before drawing plans or to get a reaction to a particular design.

34

Restrooms

The restrooms are always a great place to make an impression. First, most of your guests will use the restroom sometime during their visit to your restaurant. (HINT: Alert your staff that someone who asks the location of the restrooms is probably a first-time guest. Have them let management know at once.)

Second, many people draw a conclusion about the cleanliness of the kitchen from the cleanliness of the restrooms. Finally, using a public restroom is a very personal experience. If this experience is pleasant, it can create a lasting memory of your restaurant and give guests reasons to return.

Facial tissue   What if a guest needs to blow her nose, wipe off some makeup, clean her glasses, or do other little odd jobs? In most places, the options are only paper towels or toilet paper—not really much of a choice! Follow the example of most hotels and install a dispenser of tissues. Facial tissue is an inexpensive small touch that creates another point of difference from your competition.

Panic button   Most people will not come to you to let you know when the toilets have overflowed, and the panic button provides an alternative. A restroom "panic button" is simply a switch that turns on a flashing light somewhere else in the restaurant. A small sign asks guests to flick the switch if they see that the restroom needs attention. If you cannot hardwire the switch and light arrangement, try a wireless doorbell. The button can be on the wall in the restroom with the receiving unit near the greeter station or somewhere else that will be monitored. Have separate frequencies for each restroom and make sure someone responds at once when the buzzer sounds.

Amenities   Although restroom amenities probably have more relevance in upscale operations, anyone can add a few pleasant surprises. Unexpected touches like hand lotion, dispensed paper cups, and complimentary packets of pain reliever will reflect your concern. Consider a selection of aftershave lotions in the men's room. Amenities like a magnifying makeup mirror, a couch or flowers in the ladies room can make a big impression. A little effort in this direction and you will pick up the points even with people who don't take advantage of the amenities.

Telephones   People appreciate a private place to make a telephone call, particularly single adults. The restrooms are a perfect place to use the telephone without a date (or a would-be date) being aware of the call. Besides, restrooms are usually quieter than public hallways.

Separate table for diaper changing   If a parent has to change their child's diaper, the counter at the sink is *not* an appropriate location. A changing table can be easily wall-mounted to save space. Those who use it (and those who don't) will appreciate and remember your thoughtfulness. If you install a changing table, remember to put one in the men's room as well. Include a separate, covered waste container for the soiled diapers. For a real point bonus, have some spare disposable diapers in different sizes on hand.

An operator in one of my seminars told me she mounted the diaper changing tables on the wall in the handicapped stalls. There is always a solid wall and plenty of room that does not get utilized very often. One mother told me that it was nice to be able to close a door and strap the little guy down while she attended to her own needs. This way, when diapers are changed, it happens out of the sight of other patrons.

Full-length mirrors   If you have the wall space, place a full-length mirror in each restroom. Most people check their appearance before returning to the dining room or lounge. If they can see themselves fully, there is less chance they might be embarrassed by a detail they couldn't see in the mirror over the sink.

Style   People expect restrooms to be utilitarian. Style is an unexpected surprise! Give the same attention to decorating your restrooms as you do to decorating your restaurant and watch the compliments you get!

Fresh flowers in the ladies room might not be appropriate in a coffee shop, but a small vase of dried flowers on the counter could work. Interesting pictures on the walls or unusual light fixtures help avoid the institutional feel. If it makes your guests feel more comfortable, it is worth considering.

Restrooms also can make a statement. Consider the Madonna Inn in San Luis Obispo, California where they give tours of the men's room! Could it be something about having a 9-foot waterfall over natural rocks instead of traditional urinals?

Ice in the urinals   Have you heard about the 300-pound blocks of ice they used to put in the oversized urinals at P.J. Clarke's in New York City? The practice is over 150 years old and was the original means of sanitation. The cold kept the bacteria from growing and the slowly melting ice kept the urinals clear. In more conventional urinals, ice cubes serve the same purpose of disinfecting without chemicals. A friend who did this in his restaurant said he saved a lot on chemicals and he could always tell how long it has been since the restrooms were last checked. Plus, he said, every-body always asked about it!

Warm water in toilet tanks   How is this for attention to detail? I heard of a restaurateur who tempered the water (mixed some hot water in with the cold) in the toilet tanks in the ladies room. The idea was to make the tank water the same temperature as the room so the tanks wouldn't sweat in warm weather and the women's clothes wouldn't get wet!

Noncommercial reading material over the urinals   Read-ing material over the urinals is a nice touch. The sports or finan-cial sections of the local paper are most common (although I prefer the comics!). I am less impressed by the trend toward com-mercial ads in the restrooms. It is a source of revenue for the op-erator, but as a patron, I find it annoying. It seems to be something done for the benefit of the restaurateur rather than a service for the guest . . . but that is just one man's opinion.

Over-fixturing   Restrooms always seem to be an area that gets shorted when construction budgets get tight. If you look at restrooms as non-revenue-producing space, it is easy to justify the minimum effort. However, if you consider that exceptional restrooms, especially for the ladies, can be a major point of dif-ference between you and your competitors, the additional one-time investment might be the best money you spend.

Do more than you have to on the restrooms. If the code says you need three, put in four. If the minimum width of toilet stalls is 30 inches, make them 33 or 36 inches wide. Put in extra counter space and good quality lighting.

Having waxed philosophical about men's rooms, I should give equal time to the ladies. A few years ago, my wife and I were at the Drake Hotel in Chicago for the NRA Show. We were waiting in the lobby for some friends when someone told my wife she had to see the ladies room. Apparently the ladies rooms at the Drake are pri-vate rooms. Behind a full-length door is a toilet, sink with a stool, mirror, and lights—your own private restroom. You could do worse than being known for the greatest ladies room in town!

35

Pleasant Surprises

Perhaps this section brings us back to delight again, but you can never get too much of a good thing. Accordingly, here are a few more ideas of unexpected gestures that your guests will remember and talk to others about.

Carrying the tray   In cafeteria or buffet settings, often there are guests who have difficulty carrying their food. Whether this is due to age or injury, a service-oriented staff member will notice and offer to carry the food to the table. Even if the guest declines, the offer is noted and appreciated.

Handling special requests cheerfully   This is the application of coach Don Smith's notion that "the answer is yes, what's the question?" Not all requests can be accommodated, of course, but every one can at least be considered before a decision is made. Guests can tell when an idea is being automatically dismissed and they will resent it. If you cannot do what the guest asks, figure out how much of their request you can go along with and offer that as a possible solution. ("We just don't have the equipment necessary to actually charboil the burger. How would it be if we brushed it with liquid smoke and put it on the broiler?)

Unusual staff uniforms   This idea may have come and gone . . . which means it will probably soon be back again, but the way your staff is dressed can be something to talk about. The most extreme example of this is Bobby McGee's Conglomeration, a Phoenix-based eclectic concept. Along with the artistically cluttered interior and the salad bar in the bathtub, servers select their uniforms from what is essentially a costume shop. There are servers dressed as pirates, nurses, and who knows what else? It keeps the atmosphere humorous and seems to work for them!

You probably should not go to that extreme, but give some thought as to how you could dress your servers to make them look different from your competitors and give their look some talking power.

(Hint: Get them in on this conversation in the beginning. You will get better ideas and easier buy-in. Make a decision like this without their input and you will start a revolution!)

Hand-washing sinks in dining room   This was part of the El Puerco concept which had an interior theme that I would describe as "warehouse chic." Given the look of the place and the focus on serious barbecue, we planned to install some industrial hand-washing sinks around the dining room so guests could wash their hands without the need to go to the restrooms. I have seen this idea in place at the Bub City BBQ in Chicago, a Lettuce Entertain You venture. Even if guests do not avail themselves of the sinks, they become a tangible part of the decor and concept.

Complimentary valet parking   If your parking lot is a long way from the restaurant entrance, it may create a problem for your guests, particularly in extreme climates. Inconvenient parking can discourage business and cause your guests to get in the habit of going elsewhere. To make it as easy as possible for your guests, consider valet parking. Let the valet run down the block. Don't ask your guests to do it. If you really want to delight guests, make the valet service complimentary. After all, you don't make a cent unless guests come in to dine in the first place!

One operator told me that every car in his parking lot at lunchtime was worth $45 to him. Even if your lot is conveniently located, how many more cars could you fit in there if you were able to park them yourself?

What Do You Do for Your Guests That Your Competitors Don't?

It is never a good idea to bad-mouth the competition, but it definitely *is* in your best interests for your guests to know why you are better or different from other restaurants.

In my San Francisco restaurant, I challenged my kitchen crew to come up with a plate presentation that would elicit a spontaneous, positive comment when the plate was presented to the guest. Their response was inventive fruit garnishes—quite common now but a real rarity in the mid-1970s. When we presented the plate, we usually received a "Wow" from the guests. At that point, the server might say, "Isn't it nice to see a plate come out of a restaurant kitchen that isn't all covered with parsley!" and everyone would get a chuckle out of it.

Then, when these same people went to one of my competitors and the plate arrived (invariably) covered with parsley, they would snicker and the following exchange might occur with their tablemates:

>   A: "What's the laugh about?"
>
>   B: "Oh, it's just the parsley. It's so unimaginative. They don't do that at Crisis Hopkins."
>
>   A: "Crisis Hopkins? What's that?"
>
>   B: "Oh, it's this great new restaurant over in Embarcadero Center . . ."

They would proceed to give a commercial for my restaurant because they had plenty of things to talk about. We had created a point of difference and educated our guests about it so that they could talk to others about it. Even if they never talked to anyone else, they would at least be reminded of us whenever they saw parsley on a plate.

A little knowledge will help make sure your guests are reminded of you whenever they go to a competing restaurant!

36

Give Them the Words

If you give people the words, 75% will use them. I cannot provide hard research evidence to support that statement, but it is consistent with my experience of implementing WOM programs.

People always want something to say, and most people are not very original. Have you ever heard something on the news or read something in a magazine and later repeated the same words to someone else? Most of us have.

Perhaps we do it because we are lazy. If we trust the source, it is just easier to repeat what someone else said than it is to digest their words, sort out the meaning their message has for us, and express an original opinion. You only have to watch television news to see this "sound bite" mentality at work. Complex issues are summarized in a terse sentence, then it is on to the next story.

It is not my intent to indict contemporary thinking. As an operator, all I want is to understand how it works for people and see how I can use this insight to my advantage.

So what do you want people to say about you? If you can give them the words, you increase the odds that they will use them. When you know what you want people to talk about, develop memorable phrases to convey the message. Sound bites like "eleven secret herbs and spices" will become part of people's vocabulary if they are heard often enough from a reputable source.

Implanting Key Points of Difference

Phrases should reinforce the marketing position of your advertising. If whatever you are saying in your ads is repeated verbally to the guests when they are in your restaurant, it is more likely to stick. For example, a friend had a restaurant in Colorado called McKenna's. One of the restaurant's unique points was that they served a full menu until 1:30 in the morning.

Let's take a look at how you could give people the words. Remember, the key phrase is "McKenna's serves a full menu until 1:30 in the morning," and the goal is to find natural places to work that into the conversation.

A guest comes in after most other restaurants in the area have closed their kitchens and asks if he can get something to eat. The greeter responds cheerfully, "No problem at all. McKenna's is the only restaurant in town that serves a full menu until 1:30 in the morning. You can always get a great meal here."

Or a guest calls on the phone and asks about the operating hours. The greeter responds, "McKenna's serves a full menu until 1:30 in the morning. We are the only restaurant in town that will serve you a great meal almost anytime."

Do you see how, over time, this process would firmly connect "McKenna's" with the notion of "a full menu until 1:30 in the morning"? By adding the reference to being the only restaurant in town that does it, it further establishes the point of difference in the minds of the market.

Implanting the Name of the Restaurant

Have you ever been shopping, found something you wanted to buy, pulled out your checkbook, and had to ask the name of the store? It happens all the time.

It is entirely possible for people to stumble into your restaurant by accident, have a marvelous meal, and leave unable to recommend you because they never really knew where they were! How many times in your service sequence do you let diners know the name of your restaurant? Here are a few natural ones:

at the door:	"Welcome to McKenna's."
at the table:	"Those onion rings are one of McKenna's most popular items."
	"Have you ever tried McKenna's famous rum raisin pie?"
after dinner:	"Thank you for coming to McKenna's."

You can reinforce your name by imprinting it on cocktail napkins or napkin bands. You can put your logo on the glassware, ashtrays, and matchbooks.

Don't Count on Your Menus

You cannot count on menu copy to tell your story because people don't read menus, they scan them. In fact, people's interest in menu copy depends on their purpose for dining out. Single diners are most likely to read menus because they do not have the conversation of their table mates to occupy their time.

All that being said, it is fine to have descriptive copy on your menu. Just make sure that the key things you want people to know are presented verbally as well. If a guest is showing interest in your menu copy, be sure the server does not automatically grab the menu away when they receive the guest's order.

If you have a truly memorable body of information, you could even follow the example of Lambert's Cafe in Sikeston, Missouri and publish it all in a book! See Chapter 40 for more information.

37

Establishing a WOM Program

Okay, so you are convinced that you could do a better job of educating your guests. Where do you start? Here are my suggestions.

Identify Opportunities to Educate Guests

Review your service sequence and note where it might be possible to tell guests something about your operation. Make sure you and everyone on your crew is clear about when you could say something and have it work. Avoid situations when it will sound awkward and rehearsed.

You may want to restructure your service to provide more opportunities. For example, if the greeter's job is defined to include establishing rapport with the guest on the way to the table, you might create another natural opportunity to educate the diner as the greeter is taking him to the table.

> Greeter: Is this the first time you have been to (<u>name of restaurant</u>)?
>
> Guest: Oh no, we have been here several times.
>
> Greeter: I am so sorry not to have recognized you when you came in, Mr. _____. When was the last time you were here?
>
> Guest: It has been a couple of weeks now.
>
> Greeter: Oh! We have made a couple of interesting changes since you were here last (and proceeds to tell the guests something they didn't know).

Develop a List of Points of Difference

Your staff cannot educate your guests unless *you* educate your staff. I suggest you involve *all* staff in this discussion. Review the step-by-step progression of a guest as they dine. See what is happening and what things you might be able to talk about. Your best bet is to tap the experience and enthusiasm of your crew. They will talk about what they are genuinely excited about.

To illustrate the point figure 37-1 gives a partial list of points of difference developed for the El Puerco project.

Brief/Drill Staff on Points of Difference

Once you have a list of differences, make sure your staff knows the what and the why of them all. This is a great place for training games like "I say, you say."

Divide the staff into two groups and have a little quiz show. I say "prime rib" and the staff member responds with a "talking point"

GENERAL POINTS OF DIFFERENCE
El Puerco Border BBQ, Cosmetic Surgery & Small Engine Repair

Complimentary valet parking

Free beverages if guests have to wait

Fresh tortillas ($24K machine in display kitchen)

Fresh salsa (made in display kitchen)

House-made desserts (made in display kitchen)

Oversized wine glasses

Fresh-squeezed orange juice at the bar

Beer served in galvanized ice buckets

Free jalapeño cheese popcorn in the bar

Service guarantee – a great time every time

Choice of smaller portions at smaller prices

Choice of side dishes/desserts with entree

Wines sold based on percentage consumed

Premium well brands

Selection of reading glasses

Totally smoke-free environment

Fresh (never frozen) vegetables with entrees

Ice in the urinals

Over-fixtured restrooms

Panic button in the restrooms

Warmed water piped to the toilets (so tanks don't sweat)

Healthy menu

Diaper changing tables in each restroom

Inventive plate garnishes

Facial tissue, hand lotion in the restrooms

Full length mirrors in the restrooms

Hand-washing sinks (for guests) in the dining room

Fresh-ground premium coffee

Making a big deal out of birthdays and anniversaries

Frequent diner program

Towels instead of conventional napkins

Generous portions

Free seconds

Pass-around foods at no charge

"Warehouse chic" design

Extensive selection of non alcoholic drinks

Unique menu combination (Mexican & BBQ)

Extensive selection of appetizers

Hot food hot and cold food cold – always

Carafe service for water, iced tea, coffee

House-made soups and chilis

Items available for take-out

Reasonable prices

Smiling, outgoing staff

Memorable name

Hot towels at the beginning and end of the meal

Smaller stations for better service

Packing cases as room dividers

Picnic-table atmosphere

Extensive line of logo sportswear in gift shop

This is a partial list of the points of difference created in the concept development of the El Puerco project to be sure that staff and guests would have something to talk about. These points become part of the general training for all staff members. There are many other "talking points" in the restaurant but they would be difficult to convey without seeing the restaurant.

Figure 37-1

for the item (slow roasted, certified Angus beef, biggest selling item and so forth). Players get a point for everything they can tell you within 30 seconds about why the item you mentioned is better or different from what the competition is offering.

Alternate the questions between teams and have a meaningful prize for the winners. Better yet, find a way for everyone to win. You might say that each team gets one lottery ticket for each ten points they score with any winnings split among the team members. Use your imagination here. Your goal is to educate your staff so that they can educate your guests. Remember that your staff likes turning the guests on to something they did not know!

Monitor Interactions with Guests

The purpose of guest education is to create a personal connection with the diner by sharing information, enthusiasm, and sincerity. As the coach, you need to listen to what is being said at the table. In particular, watch for excessive repetition and staleness. The seventeenth time a server says the same line, it will start sounding rehearsed and impersonal.

Coach as Necessary

When you identify staleness, suggest they find other things to talk about for awhile. If servers are not talking, find out why and repeat the training if necessary. If servers are not sincere in what they are saying, you must identify it and help them get back on track.

Have a Good Time

People come to restaurants expecting to have a good time. The more fun the staff and management is having, the easier it is for the guests to enjoy themselves. I do not mean to suggest that the restaurant staff conduct themselves like second graders at recess, but beware of getting too serious. Oh yes, and if you are having a good time, notify your face!

38

What Makes a WOM Program Work?

Please don't think that wishing will make it so when it comes to WOM. If you are just going through the motions, guests will pick up on that and it can actually work against you. To help flesh out the process a bit more, here are a few thoughts on the factors that will help assure the success (or guarantee the failure) of a WOM program.

Human Factors

Perhaps the most important element is trust. Guests have to be able to count on you to deliver on your promises every time. Trust is fragile—it takes a long time to build and it can be lost in a moment of inattention. Did you ever have a car that didn't start every time? How many times did that happen before you started looking for a new car? That is the result when you lose trust. If you have a strong personal relationship with the diners they may continue to patronize you, but they will not take the chance of recommending you to their friends if they cannot be sure what sort of experience their friends will have.

The qualities in your staff that bear on the success of your WOM program are sincerity, enthusiasm, and naturalness. In other words, people have to believe what your crew is saying. There is a certainty in the voice that guests can detect and it will not come from scripted communication. "Do you want fries with that" is a chant. "Ooh! You have *got* to try our new cheese fries!" is a sincere personal recommendation. When the personal connection is made, it is a gift of hospitality and friendship. Guests must truly sense that your overriding concern is for them, not for yourself.

Finally, you must be sure to give people the words. People are likely to say to others what they hear you saying to them. Memorable phrases are often created spontaneously. When one of these gems drops in your lap, remember it and alert others on the staff to it.

Share stories of what has been working. An interesting exercise in staff meetings is to explore how various servers have been telling guests about a particular item or feature. It gets the crew more involved in the operation and expands the general knowledge base. You might learn a few things in the process!

Service Staff Selection Criteria

The easiest way to support an on-going WOM program is to hire people who can get excited and give them things that are worth getting excited about! Not every person who applies for a job will be effective at supporting a WOM program even though he or she may otherwise be an efficient server.

You must look for workers with expressive movement—people with a tendency to wave their arms around, move their faces, and smile from the heart. Stiff, stone-faced servers will not be able to engage the guests or effectively convey excitement and enthusiasm. You want people with a sense of humor who can laugh at themselves and involve guests in the fun.

Mike Hurst of 15th Street Fisheries has a simple test to judge the expressiveness of applicants. At the end of the interview, he assumes a serious demeanor and with a straight face asks the applicant, "What's the funniest thing that ever happened to you?" He is looking for the spontaneous smile, not the good story (although a good story is a plus)! If candidates get serious and give some intellectual answer, they are not going to work out. Candidates who break into a big grin and can laugh at themselves under these circumstances has a good chance of delivering the enthusiasm and sincerity that will make a WOM program successful.

Market Factors

The points you raise with your guests must address factors that are important to the guest. People are concerned about quality, freshness, and things that make the meal special—points that will make them seem intelligent and informed when they pass them along to others. They are not likely to be interested in the fact that your meat comes packed in Cryovac! For every point you consider sharing with your guests, ask yourself, "So what?" If you do not have a good answer to the question, drop the item from your repertoire.

The other effective market factor is anything that will help you create points of difference from the competition. What are you doing that is better or different? What can they get with you that they cannot get anywhere else? This addresses the need to educate people as to why they come to you and to give them reasons to think of you when they go to another restaurant.

Operational Criteria

To deliver a consistent WOM program you must have a credible operation. All the tricks in the world will not work if you are not doing things that are truly worth talking about or if your execution is haphazard. Trust comes from consistency and sincerity. So you have to be a good restaurant that guests can count on. They have to know that you always have the best interests of your patrons at heart.

Finally, it is important to involve your staff in all aspects of the operation. When the staff is involved, they refer to things in terms of "us" and "we." When they are not an integral part of the planning process, their phrases tend to include "they" and "them" when referring to the restaurant. Patrons notice the difference.

39

What Will Not Work?

It is important to understand that WOM is an attitude and an approach, not a technique. The ideas outlined in this section will work for you but only if they are executed properly. If your heart is not in the right place, the factors we have discussed will come across as hollow and insincere. They will actually work against you. Knowing what helps a WOM program succeed may automatically alert you to what will keep it from working, but we should review the points briefly to be sure.

Human factors   Any kind of scam or con will turn guests away. In the same way, scripted communications ("Hi. My name is Karen and I will be your server tonight") only show insincerity and lack of personal interest. Any time the server—or the manager for that matter—is focused on his or her own interests rather than the interests of the guest, it will hurt rapport and trust. Using WOM as a technique is dangerous.

Market factors   There is nothing to be gained by addressing obscure points. If you confuse the guests or tell them things they cannot easily grasp, they will not be effective spokespersons for you. In fact, if you lose the guests' interest or talk about things they can't understand, they may feel uncomfortable and decide not to return. Keep it simple.

Addressing points that are overexposed in the market is also dangerous. The "me too" approach will only make you look silly. For example, if a competitor mounts a successful promotion for alligator appetizers, don't advertise that you have alligator. It will only remind potential diners of the competition.

Finally, running down the competition will hurt you. Your goal is to educate guests as to why you are better or different, not why the competition is worse. They can figure that out for themselves. Be competitive but don't strive to compete—strive to excel. Find unique products and services that you can be the first to bring to the market. Rudyard Kipling is quoted as saying, "They copied and copied and copied, but they couldn't copy my mind. So I left them sweating and stealing, a year and a half behind."

Imitation may be the sincerest form of flattery. Just be sure that competitors are copying you and not the other way around.

Operational Factors

Leaving WOM to chance is suicidal. You cannot count on guests to know what you have done for them unless you tell them about it. This means that you have to educate your staff so that they will get excited and educate your guests. When people are not talking about a restaurant, it is more likely the result of failing to structure a WOM program and failing to train the crew than it is that there was nothing in the restaurant to talk about.

Inconsistency will kill a WOM program quickly. If something interesting happens one time and not the next, if the portion sizes change or the taste of the product varies, it costs you the trust of your patrons. When guests stop trusting you, they will not take a chance on recommending you to others. They might even stop coming back themselves.

Finally, if you do not offer anything that is special or different, there will be nothing for people to talk about. This is not to suggest that you drop all your basic menu items and get wildly avant garde; that is more likely to confuse your guests than to delight them. But see what you can do to put an interesting twist on familiar items.

There isn't much you can say that will make anything special of plain french toast made from white sandwich bread served with table syrup. If you try to talk it up, you will just look ridiculous to the guests when they get their order.

But what if you offered "thick-cut cinnamon raisin french toast" served with real Vermont maple syrup? Now you (and your guests) really have something special to talk about! The item is different but not confusing, easy to describe to the guest and easy for the guest to describe to others.

40

Lambert's: A Case Study

I have mentioned Lambert's Cafe in Missouri several times. Lambert's has done a better-than-the-average job of structuring themselves in a way that gives their guests plenty to talk about. They have been the subject of nationally syndicated articles appearing in newspapers in all 50 states and countless international media reports.

Here is just one of many, in this case from the Memphis Commercial Appeal. See how much the writer has to work with and how the article itself could generate additional word-of-mouth:

Cafe Society Likes Mules, Thrown Rolls
Commentary by Rheta Grimsley Johnson

James Arness, Elvis and Clint Eastwood have all chowed down at Lambert's Cafe. And if Eastwood had said, "Make my day," or for that matter, "Kiss my foot," somebody would have thrown a roll at him. Rest assured.

That's what Lambert's is famous for. "Throwed rolls."

Owner Norman Lambert and the rest of the waiters throw rolls at everybody, not discriminating for age, sex, creed, color or celebrity.

On May 26, 1976, Norman was pushing a cart of his popular homemade rolls around the dining room and a customer got impatient for service. "Throw me one," the customer said.

Norman did. He liked it. The customer liked it. The cash register liked it.

Soon Norman was perfecting his pitch and hefting hot rolls all over the place. The television and newspapers picked up on it. Reporters are always anxious for what's known affectionately in the trade as a "lite-n-brite," some catchy something for tense Dan Rather to smile about at the end of his telecast. So the reporters wrote and talked about it.

And soon people started driving from miles around to get food thrown at them. Norman's pitch became his pitch. Home of the "throwed roll" became his slogan. The little cafe that Norman's father and mother started on a $1,500 loan in 1942 became regionally famous. It outgrew its nine stools and eight tables and strictly local emphasis.

You cannot fault the place for relying on a single gimmick to draw customers. It does not. Anyone who can stand the noise level will get food to eat, all of it good, make no mistake.

A piped-in medley by Danny Davis and the Nashville Brass will instill the first three measures of 32 down home hits in your head forever, or at least until you wash it out with a good dose of rock.

Even the best medley is a taunt: by the time you are ready to hum along, some smart aleck changes songs. The green, green grass of I can't stop loving you. It makes you want to throw a hot roll at the speakers.

This is the perfect restaurant for those who love to eat, don't care who sees them do it and who don't mind screaming children, popping balloons, flying rolls, magic tricks during a meal and hearing the same brief part of the same songs over and over.

It is not a good restaurant for honeymooners who want a nice, romantic, candlelight dinner; for snotty food critics who sniff wines, or for pretentious sorts who took three quarters of French and think they know the food and language. This is more like crashing a children's birthday party in McDonald's, where the only French you are likely to encounter is a fry stuck in your ear.

But Lambert's is fun, if not for a steady diet. Waiters are fabulously attentive, bringing by buckets of hot food you did not order and adding it to the already heaping portions on your plate. The white beans, red pepper relish, slaw, fried potatoes, cooked apples and rolls bigger than softballs are all extra. No charge.

The only way to lose your appetite along with your waist-line is to read some of Lambert's literature, which brags that the flatulence level from the 20,800 pounds of white beans served last year could power a city, or notes that the restaurant used 42,000 sheets of toilet paper a week and just 23,700 napkins.

There is also the matter of the mules on the wall. Norman collects mule pictures. So while you are spared the fake country motif so popular these days—rusted snuff signs, horse collars and other cutesy interpretations of life behind a split-rail—there are plenty of pretty pictures to occupy the eye while the mouth works.

Or, objects d'art, some would say.

But then nobody says that kind of things here. It is mules, not jackasses, that Lambert's specializes in.

How do I know all this about Lambert's? Well from a humorous little 48-page book that they sell in the restaurant's gift shop! *Sell*, mind you, and they sell a lot of them! The book includes several articles like this along with original cartoons and statistics with "talking power." Here is just one example:

"Hog Jowl"

Once we just served jowl for breakfast but for the past year we have offered it on our dinner menu. What a response hog jowl received. We now serve over 399 pounds per week or 20,785 pounds a year. It's sugar cured and aged to perfection and to just be honest—bacon just "don't" compare. Try it on your next visit.

What could you be doing that would be so interesting that people would pay to find out more about it?

41

El Puerco: A Case Study

Throughout this section, I have mentioned elements from the El Puerco concept that I created for an operator in Colorado. Although the owner was ultimately unable to raise the funds necessary to implement the concept, El Puerco was a project totally created with an eye toward developing positive word-of-mouth as a way to maximize sales and as such might be a helpful model to illustrate some of the points in this section.

Figure 37-1 is a partial list of the points of difference created in the concept development of the El Puerco project to be sure that staff and guests would have something to talk about. These points become part of the general training for all staff members as discussed in this section.

There are many other "talking points" in the restaurant besides the items listed. There are physical points of difference and unique design elements that would be difficult to convey without presenting plans and renderings of the restaurant. In the interests of space, I have not attempted to describe differences in menu structure or the unique recipes because grasping their relevance would depend on understanding the competitive climate in the market area.

While guests tend not to read them, menus can still be an effective place to provide guest information. To illustrate one way to do this, Figure 41-1 offers the text from the back of the El Puerco menu. If the spirit of the words strikes you, then use it as a model to develop notions that are unique to your own operation.

EL PUERCO PROMISES

1. This restaurant is run for the enjoyment and pleasure of our guests, not the convenience of the staff or the owners. We guarantee that you will have a great time every time you come here, we will earn your trust and your enthusiastic endorsement, and we will never disappoint you or your friends.

2. This is a completely smoke-free restaurant. We realize this may be an inconvenience to some of our guests and we are truly sorry for that. If you are reading this, you have decided to give us a try and we promise that your experience at El Puerco will be worth a few extra minutes of "cold turkey"!

3. Aside from smoking in our restaurant, the answer is yes! What's the question?

4. You'll never hear us ask "Is everything OK?" When we pose questions, they will be more thoughtful than that!

5. We think it is fair to sell at a price greater than our cost in an effort to stay in business! However, we will never sacrifice quality just to keep prices low. If we can't do it right, we won't do it at all.

6. We use only Maverick Ranch Lite Beef®, the official beef supplier to the U.S. Olympic teams. It has less calories than chicken, about the same fat level as fish and contains no chemicals. We are the only restaurant in Colorado that can offer you this exceptional product. Enjoy!

7. Ask us for our recommendations. You'll never be told that "everything is good here." We don't consider this response, however accurate, to be particularly helpful as a recommendation.

8. We cook all our "fried foods" in hot air. We don't even *own* a deep fat fryer! The equipment to do this is more expensive, but we think you can taste and appreciate the difference. When we *do* use oil, we use only cholesterol-free olive or canola oil. Please ask how any item is prepared. We can tell you!

9. We have a selection of reading glasses if you forgot yours. It's *hell* when you pass 40, isn't it?!

10. Your server will at least say hello within one minute after you are seated or your desserts are on us.

11. We use only premium coffees and always grind our coffee beans just before we brew. We never, ever let a pot sit longer than 30 minutes. We will not serve you that "toasty" coffee at El Puerco.

12. You will get all necessary condiments before we serve your meal. We won't make you wait with your food getting cold while we get our act together!

13. We will not greet you with a question ("Two?"). When you first enter our restaurant, someone will actually smile at you and thank you for coming. We really are glad that you're here!

14. We strive to be environmentally responsible. We bale all our cardboard, minimize our use of chemicals and recycle whatever we can. Our take-out containers contain no CFC's. It's a start.

15. We serve hot food hot and cold food cold. Period.

16. We are proud of the cleanliness of our restrooms. We check them every half hour to be sure, but you know how quickly accidents can happen. If you find the restrooms need attention, push the "Panic Button" on the restroom wall or tell anyone on our staff. We will correct the problem at once.

17. Substitutions and special requests are fine with us. Don't be bashful about letting us know exactly what you want.

18. We make a big deal out of birthdays and anniversaries. If you don't want some attention, don't let on that you are celebrating a special occasion.

19. We formulate all our recipes to be ① delicious, ② lower in fat and cholesterol and ③ lower in sodium. A complete nutritional analysis of all our recipes is available if you're interested. Just ask.

20. We will listen to you. We will find out what you want, how you want it and we will give it to you just that way. If for some reason we blow it, just stand up and yell "HELP!" That'll fix us!

Menu copy from the El Puerco Border BBQ, Cosmetic Surgery & Small Engine Repair

Figure 41-1

Provide Incentives
to Return

42

Incentives Work

The simple premise behind incentive programs is that people do what they are rewarded for doing. If you want water, you have to prime the pump, and if you want guests to return, it helps to give them incentives to do so. ("I do this because . . .")

Incentives fall into three general categories:

Discounts include business card drawings, bounce-back coupons, and meal period discounts like early bird specials.

Promotions are targeted for specific events created either by the guest or by the restaurant. These include birthdays, anniversaries, holidays, special events, and festivals.

Customer Loyalty Programs reward guests for repeat patronage. These take the form of punch cards, point systems, and percentage plans.

Let's take a look at these in more detail.

43

Discounts

Most operators cringe at the word "discount" as visions of declining profits, piles of coupons, and "two-fer" deals elevate the heart rate and bring on cold sweats. Relax. If you get nervous about discounts, it may be just that you are not seeing them the same way I am.

In the parlance of GBM, *a discount is a deal for the guest that generates more profit for the operator.*

How can a deal be more profitable? When it creates a sale that you would otherwise not have received. It helps to remind yourself that you pay bills with dollars, not percentages. Here is a quick quiz question taken from *The Foolproof Foodservice Selection System* that illustrates the point:

> All other things being equal, which one of the following items would you encourage your staff to sell?
>
> A. An enchilada plate selling for $6.95 with a 20% food cost.
>
> B. A chicken sandwich selling for $4.95 with a 32% food cost.
>
> C. A fried catfish platter selling for $8.95 with a 38% food cost.
>
> D. A steak dinner selling for $12.95 with a 50% food cost.

The answer is D—a steak dinner selling for $12.95 with a 50% food cost. While the steak has the highest food cost percentage, its gross margin (the amount of money you get to keep every time you sell it) is $6.48. Gross margin on the other choices is as follows: enchiladas, $5.56; chicken sandwich, $3.37, and catfish, $5.55.

I firmly believe that you should never discount your basic product. If the steak dinner is a signature item for you at $12.95, how can you offer it for half price with a coupon and ever expect to sell it at full price again without your guests questioning what it is really worth?

So I suggest that any offers representing a dollar savings to guests never touch your signature items. However, you can more safely offer a price break on appetizers, desserts, drinks, and other discretionary products. For example, you can offer free appetizers to parties of four or 50% off desserts after 9:30 p.m. . . . and you can more safely make this offer to those who have already graced you with their patronage.

In the example above, let's say that you offered a free dessert to everyone who ordered the steak. If you normally sold the dessert for $3.50 and your cost on the item was 80 cents, have you hurt yourself?

When you sell the steak, you make $6.48 in gross margin. Giving away the dessert lowers that to $5.68 ($6.48 less the 80-cent cost of the dessert). Looking at your other menu items, you receive only $5.56 in gross margin when you sell an enchilada plate or $5.55 from a catfish plate (at full price!). A discount offer like this represents a tremendous value to the guest (they are getting a $3.50 dessert for "free") and does not really cost you anything more than if they had ordered enchiladas or catfish.

Now some readers will protest that the house has lost the $2.50 gross margin it would have had from the dessert sale. If every guest ordered dessert every time, that might be true. But if 20% of your guests typically order dessert, you only had a one in five chance of the dessert sale to start with, so the "risk" is more like 50 cents in lost margin.

However, if the offer stimulated a sale from a guest who would otherwise have stayed home or gone to a competitor, the net impact on your bottom line is quite positive.

People do what they are rewarded for.

44

Business Card Drawings

Many restaurants have a fishbowl at the front desk where they ask people to deposit their business cards for some sort of monthly drawing. The prize is often products or services at the restaurant like dinner for two or a bottle of wine with dinner. The incentive could also be merchandise bartered with a local business. For example, the restaurant might trade meals for a leather briefcase and offer the case as a prize.

Most operators use the cards to develop a mailing list (and it is certainly helpful to be able to make offers directly to past guests); however, I doubt if many have thought about how to use business cards as a form of GBM.

In fact, business cards can be effectively used to generate repeat business if you use them properly. Here is an example.

Big Spenders

I had a variation on the business card drawing when I had Crisis Hopkins, my first restaurant in San Francisco. We had a special clear plastic box made and mounted it by the front door. We encouraged guests to deposit their business cards for what we called our "Big Spenders" drawing. At 4:00 every weekday afternoon we selected one card and posted it in a special holder on the front of the box.

Anyone who worked for the company selected (i.e., had a business card from the company) could buy drinks for half price that afternoon. In other words, they got to act like "Big Spenders." Even if they wanted to buy a round for the house (nobody ever did), they could do it at half price. Since Crisis was the "hot bar" in town at the time, this was definitely a worthwhile prize!

However, there was only one way to find out who the big spenders of the day were—you had to come into the restaurant and check the box. We would never reveal the winning card over the phone. These rules made Crisis Hopkins the first place people headed when they got off work. If you were going to have a drink before heading home, why not see if you could get it at half price, right? Once people were in the restaurant, they usually stayed. We made the money and our competitors never got the chance to win them over.

Now some cost-focused readers may be worried about the financial impact of selecting a card from a large local employer, so let me share a story about that.

Crisis Hopkins was located in the financial district of San Francisco. At the time, Levi Strauss, the clothing maker, was headquartered on the top ten floors of the building immediately above us.

Whenever we would draw a Levi Strauss business card, it was fun to watch. Someone from Levi would wander in about 4:30 in the afternoon, see that Levi Strauss folks were the "big spenders" that day, and ask to use our phone. They would call upstairs and tell everyone to get down to Crisis immediately! The upper floors would empty and the Levi mob would carry on until after 9:00 that night!

All those people at 50% off! It broke my heart! The bar was always crowded, which helped our image and drew others to "where the action was!" People like to be where other people are.

Sure, we let the Levi crew buy drinks at half price that day . . . but we still made a little on each drink and they bought a lot of drinks! Better yet, all of the Levi folks—people in my prime market—got in the habit of coming to my restaurant after work. They became accustomed to having a great time in my place and we made money from their patronage. In fact, we made it a point to "randomly" draw a Levi Strauss card at least every other month, usually on a Monday or Tuesday!

45

Internal Coupons

External couponing is out of control in many segments of the foodservice market. Increased competition has driven many operators to flood the market with widespread couponing in direct mail pieces, newspapers, magazines, and other mass marketing means. While this may produce a temporary increase in guest counts, there is no clear opinion whether the practice is profitable or even desirable in the long run.

The role of couponing in GBM is limited to offers that are extended only to existing restaurant guests. They are typically special offers to encourage repeat patronage, not (particularly) price discounts, although a price break may be included to encourage the return visit.

Internal coupons can take a variety of different forms. The three most common are outlined below.

Courtesy Coupons

These are pocket-sized coupons that all members of the restaurant staff carry—essentially blank checks that they can issue to guests for use on a return visit. Courtesy coupons may be appropriate if the guest has a complaint or is inconvenienced by something. They can also be used to reward guests for past patronage or to encourage a guest to return.

You can accomplish all these goals with your existing gift certificates, but courtesy coupons are faster to issue and easier to use. The guest does not have to wait while someone rummages around in the office looking for the key to the gift certificate box!

Cross-Marketing Coupons

These coupons might be used in a restaurant with a particularly strong meal period to encourage return visits during slower meal periods. For example, a downtown restaurant might make an offer to luncheon patrons that can be redeemed during dinner hours. A suburban dinner house might want to provide an incentive for weekend guests to return on a Monday or Tuesday evening. (This could be a great place for that "free dessert when you order a steak" idea we discussed in Chapter 43.)

Companion Coupons

This is an offer sent to regular patrons that encourages them to return to the restaurant with a friend. A companion coupon might offer a free bottle of wine for a party of four or a specially priced line of entrees designed to be shared between two people.

Companion coupons can also be designed to be given to a friend by the patron who receives them. For example, Warren's Lobster House in Kittery, Maine recently sent picture postcards to the members of their frequent diner club. The postcards were preprinted invitations to visit the restaurant for a free appetizer with dinner. The intention was that the restaurant's FDP members sent these cards to their colleagues. The sender got to do a favor for a friend and the restaurant gained exposure to new patrons. Dave Mickee, Warren's co-owner, reports mixed results from this one, perhaps because guests did not fully understand the idea he had in mind. He says many just mailed the cards to themselves and brought them in . . . but at least they came back in!

46

Meal Period Discounts

These are price breaks to encourage guests to dine at off-peak hours. Typically, the goal has been to build business in the early part of the evening when the restaurant is slow, but some operators are finding that there is business to be built at other times of the day (or night) as well.

These discounts fit into the framework of GBM if they are not advertised to the public. Word is spread strictly by word of mouth by existing guests. This process might be a bit slower but it is less expensive and far more effective. Remember that people like to know things that others do not and letting them in on a "secret" can work big dividends.

Early Bird Specials

Mike Hurst at 15th Street Fisheries in Fort Lauderdale, Florida has elevated the early bird to an art form. His early bird runs from 5:00 p.m.–5:15 p.m. and offers a $5 discount off the price of a dinner entree (Mike runs a good average check!). Perhaps because his market area has so many retired folks who are looking for a deal, Mike reports that his dining room is packed at 5:15 every night! It is a great way to jump-start the evening's sales. It is also the biggest hit the kitchen will get all evening and makes the rest of the night, no matter how busy, look easy by comparison!

Late Night Specials

Sometimes called an "owly bird," the same idea can apply to late night dining. How about offering a discount for guests who come in after your main dinner rush is over? The kitchen is fired up, the staff is on hand, and you have the seats sitting empty. The times during which you might make such an offer will vary with the operation, the flow of business, and the time of the year, but this can be very profitable additional business.

A successful example of developing the late night trade comes from Nashville, Tennessee. Randy Rayburn at Sunset Grill has instituted a late night menu that has come to exceed lunch as a source of revenue. Best of all, he has accomplished this without expending a penny in advertising.

His late night menu consists of some lower food cost entrees off his regular menu and any items he wants to run out. These entrees are offered at half price from 10:00 p.m. until 1:30 a.m. during the week and from midnight until 1:30 p.m. on Saturday night. Desserts, coffees, and beverages remain at full menu price. His late night sales mix is about equally divided between food and beverages. Because of its structure, he reports that the late night menu only runs about four points higher in overall food cost than his regular menu.

Randy says that a large percentage of his late night market has become restaurant people looking for a bite to eat in different surroundings when they get off work! His staff makes it a point to inform guests about the late night deal and they, in turn, pass the word along to others. The late night menu takes a smaller kitchen staff to produce, and all his managers are cross-trained on pantry operations in case a kitchen worker calls in sick.

Interestingly, Randy discontinued his early bird program when the late night menu took off. It seemed that the market could think of Sunset Grill either as a place to go early or as a place to go late . . .

but not both. This is something to think about when considering what sort of programs to implement in your operation.

In Randy's case, he preferred the later business. His early evening business was building up well without any additional incentives and he found that his early diners were not particularly price-driven.

47

Promotions

Promotions are an important element in building repeat patronage because they give guests a reason to return. ("I go there because _____.) There are a variety of promotion styles. We have all seen the highly advertised special events that some of the major restaurant chains run from time to time. This may be practical for them but it is definitely out of the question for the typical independent operator.

I question the wisdom of this sort of wide-ranging effort in any case. It may get the message to thousands of people, but how many of them are ever likely to come to your restaurant regardless of the offer?

So the promotions in GBM are centered on your existing guests. If a diner had not already been to your restaurant, most of these sales-builders would be impossible. In fact, these promotions are all the more powerful when they are not advertised outside the restaurant.

This approach decreases the quantity of the potential market but it greatly increases the quality—the percentage of people that you are likely to capture. I suspect that, in the end, the measure of a promotion is how much business it brings in, how much good will it creates, and (perhaps) how much net profit it produces. The range of a promotion's geographic reach may be good for the ego but seldom puts money in your pocket.

In the following chapters, we will look at several natural promotions that most every restaurant can execute successfully to increase the number of times guests come in.

Specifically, we will look at the following opportunities:

Birthdays and Anniversaries

Holidays

Special Events

Festivals

Remember that the primary value of a promotion in a GBM program is that it gives you a reason to invite guests to return . . . and it gives them a reason to do it. If the promotion gets a guest back just one more time during the month, it will be successful.

A secondary value is that promotions break up the daily routine for your guests and your staff. Promotions give you a reason to do something different—try new recipes, change the look of the place, experiment with different types of services, or just do something silly. When the promotion is over, the restaurant is never exactly the same as it was before. Keeping the feeling of freshness is important to your long-term success.

48

Birthdays and Anniversaries

Every couple will have at least three significant events a year that typically call for dining out—each partner's birthday and their wedding anniversary. You can get these dates when people join your frequent diner plan or simply place a poster in the lobby inviting people to sign up for your birthday club. Once you know these dates, it is a perfectly natural time to invite them to return to the restaurant to celebrate with you.

The biggest mistake I have seen in this regard is to make a birthday and anniversary offer that is only valid on the significant day itself. You will do better to cut the guest some slack and loosen up the redemption period on your offer. For example, The Board Room BBQ in Overland Park, Kansas keeps track of customers' birthdays and sends cards offering a free entree anytime during the month of a customer's birthday. The redemption rate is 75%.

If your operation is a quick service or family-style operation, you will probably lose out to more upscale options on the day of the special occasions. If you take your mate to a drive-in burger joint for your tenth wedding anniversary, there may not be an eleventh!

So how can a quick service or family restaurant take advantage of birthdays and anniversaries?

Let's say that I own a Mom-and-Pop place called "Bill's Diner"—the sort of restaurant with a regular eggs and coffee morning crowd and a modest check average. I would certainly invite my guests to come in for a special deal sometime during the month of their birthday or anniversary. I might even send them a "Happy Birthday" coupon they could use anytime at their convenience. After all, I want to keep them coming back. However, I would not expect them to celebrate the special day with me. (In fact, I will gladly give that business away to be the place they come to twice a week!)

But if the celebrants were regular patrons of mine, I would also make it a point to find out where they intended to go on the special day itself. When they sat down to dinner at "La Splendido," there would be a bottle of wine (or complimentary desserts) along with a card signed by all the staff at my restaurant. "Happy anniversary from your friends at Bill's Diner." So as they sit in a competitor's restaurant and celebrate, they are talking about the incredible people at Bill's Diner!

It is an intensely personal gesture—a gift to them with no immediate benefit to the giver—and they will love it! What do you bet that they will return to Bill's at least once to say thank you? That one visit alone will pay for the cost of the wine. Better yet, the gesture will create a more personal connection with Bill's Diner and further solidify the long-term relationship.

Even if you do not buy a gift at a competitor's restaurant, what would it take to send a card, signed by everyone on the staff, to acknowledge the special occasion? If you have a large mailing list, it may be hard to stay ahead of this but the impact is worth the effort. You may have a retiree in the area or a former staff member at home with small children who would enjoy a little part-time work. You might be able to trade meals for services rendered.

There are companies with huge automated machines who will handle the mailing task for you. While this is more effective than doing nothing, it is certainly more impersonal than a hand-addressed card, particularly one filled with staff members' signatures and personal wishes.

It is fine to have a policy about what you will do for parties celebrating special occasions but for maximum impact, your invitation and your offer must be personal. Remember, the hospitality business is based on personal connection.

Many restaurants will provide a small complimentary cake to guests who are celebrating a special occasion. While it is amazing how many "birthdays" some people can have in a year, don't worry about the people who will take advantage of your generosity. They still have dinner, they still buy wine . . . and it is one less chance your competition has to make an impression on them!

49

Holidays

The powerful aspect of holidays is that they are well-advertised . . . by other people! You do not need to tell your guests that Easter is coming or that Thanksgiving will soon be upon you. It is everywhere.

As it relates to GBM, holidays are a natural time to invite guests to return for a special meal or a special offer. The offer can be presented in posters in the lobby, flyers included with the guest check, or direct mailing to your existing diners.

Where can you get your guests' addresses for a mailing? Well, you will certainly have the addresses of members of your frequent diner plan. If you take telephone numbers when guests make a dinner reservation, you can consult a reverse telephone directory to locate the name and address of the caller. Business card drawings and comment cards can be a source of guests' addresses for your mailing list.

There is presently a system called Guestbook developed by Plainfield Software of Portland, Oregon that can allow you to place a small computer terminal in the lobby of your restaurant. With an on-screen graphic display, the terminal itself encourages guests to enter their own information directly into your database, asks them questions regarding their particular interests (For example, "Are you interested in winemaker dinners?"), and rewards them with a random gift for their efforts. Users report as high as a 60% response rate on mailings to people who have indicated their interest in particular events. (See "Resources" on page 203.)

A special offer does not have to be a price reduction in order to draw guests back. Often, the most effective offers can be a package of goods and services actually priced higher than your regular check average. For example, Thanksgiving dinner including wine, dessert, and a package of leftover turkey to take home for sandwiches would be something delightfully different that could easily command a higher price. Remember that people pay for *value* received more than for *product* received.

In your planning, consider the fact that not all "holidays" are officially designated as such. The highest volume day in many restaurants is Mother's Day, not a holiday but an occasion that certainly deserves a special offer. Father's Day, Valentine's Day, and so forth are all opportunities to make an offer and invite your guests to take you up on it.

Ethnic restaurants can celebrate not only U.S. holidays but the holidays related to their country of origin. For example, Mexican cantinas can get mileage from Cinco de Mayo, French restaurants can put on an annual Bastille Day bash, and the Venice International Film Festival could provide an opportunity for an Italian eatery to make a special offer.

Whatever the occasion, holiday celebrations give you an excuse to invite guests back that one additional time a month.

50

Special Events

Special events are a part of GBM when they are only promoted to the present and past guests of the restaurant. The word goes out through verbal prompts from the service staff, posters in the lobby, flyers included with the guest checks, and mentions in the restaurant's newsletter.

Special events can either be a regular occurrence on a particular day of the week or month or something that only happens once a year. In general, they are not promoted to the public at large through media advertising. This limits the potential audience but it saves a lot of money—savings that can be re-invested into creating a more spectacular event.

If the event promotion is only done through internal sources, it also gives your regulars a "secret" they can share with their friends. Remember that people love to know things that other people don't know. In fact, special events should be designed to encourage present patrons to bring in new people to join them for a unique evening.

Events that only last for a day should have a limited number of seats available. Nothing is a more powerful endorsement of a program than a waiting list. Send a consolation note to those who never make it off the list, inviting them to your next event.

If an event is a once-a-year occasion or if it carries a high price tag, print a special invitation and mail it to your regulars. The members of your frequent diner plan are obvious choices to hear of special events before you make the information available to other guests in the restaurant. Your regulars expect this sort of preferential treatment and it is an additional incentive for folks to become members of your FDP.

Depending on the event, think about structuring it in such a way that you can make the event price all-inclusive. Many people like to pay one amount up front without having to worry about tax and tip.

Special events can take a limitless variety of forms. Here are a few examples to start your thought processes.

Cigar dinners   It is interesting to note that as cigarette smoking in restaurants is becoming less prevalent, cigar dinners are turning out to be one of the hottest restaurant events in the country. These are typically upscale events that combine fine cigars with fine wines and spirits, usually at a hefty tab. If such an event would fit for your restaurant, *Cigar Aficionado* magazine has a cigar dinner event planner that is a must-read. Information on how to contact them is included in the Resources chapter on page 203.

Wine-centered events   Winemaker dinners are popular in many restaurants. These events are co-sponsored with the winery where the restaurant offers a special menu and attendees get to sample a variety of wines from that winery and discuss them with the winemaker.

Wine tastings can also be held as special events, although these are more likely to work as a regular monthly activity rather than a once-a-year occurrence. Wine tastings are usually a paid event where participants sample several different wines and learn something about them. This is a perfect opportunity to showcase the knowledge of your wine list manager and boost future wine sales. Hold the tastings in the early evening on a slower night of the week so the attendees can stay for dinner after the event.

I did a variation on this idea when I wanted to change the house wine at Crisis Hopkins, my San Francisco restaurant. Rather than having the management team make the decision, we turned it into an event—a blind tasting of jug wines to select the new house pour. Our rationale was that our guests' opinion was what ultimately determined how well the wine would go over, so why not let them make the decision in the first place?

We created The Great White Wine Tasting Team and invited thirty of our regular patrons to participate as official team members. We promoted it only in the restaurant and the event drew quite a crowd. We charged bystanders to taste and comment, although the official team had the responsibility for the final selection.

We designed a logo (Figure 50-1), made t-shirts for all the participants, and had a local celebrity as a guest taster. We took a team photo that later hung in the restaurant and spent two days sipping wines that we (management) had determined we could live with price-wise. When it was all over, the team actually selected the least expensive wine in the contest! We had a lot of fun, drew a lot of folks to the restaurant, and gave people plenty to talk about!

T-shirt Tuesday   Stan Clark of Eskimo Joe's in Stillwater, Oklahoma has probably done the best job of clothing merchandising

Figure 50-1

of any independent restaurateur I know. While perhaps not on the level of a Hard Rock Cafe or Planet Hollywood, Joe's has a 28-page, four-color catalog that is sent out three times a year to a mailing list of over 175,000 people!

One of Stan's best recurring promotions is T-shirt Tuesday where anyone wearing an Eskimo Joe's t-shirt gets draft beer for a dime! Since Stillwater is the home of Oklahoma State University, you *know* that one of a new student's first stops is Eskimo Joe's to buy a t-shirt! Stan takes a bit of a hit on his pouring costs every time he runs this, but he packs the place and sells a lot of food! Plus, he gets the advertising value of thousands of students walking around campus advertising his restaurant!

Restaurant birthday party   It's hard enough to keep a restaurant in business, so when you make it through another year, it is a good reason to invite a few people by to celebrate! Eskimo Joe's has also elevated this to an art form. Their annual birthday party has become a state-wide media event that draws tens of thousands of people to the restaurant's parking lot and generates 2–3 days of TV news coverage. The police have to close off the street and it is the largest public gathering in Stillwater outside of OSU football games! What are you doing to celebrate *your* restaurant's birthday?

Charity fundraisers   Nothing does good like doing good. Local charities always need money and restaurants always need exposure and business. Planning a special event to benefit a local charity can pay off for everyone.

A charity fundraiser only means that you give some of the proceeds to a worthy cause, not that the event has to be a break-even venture for you. Your willingness to share in this highly visible manner improves your image in the market and helps set you apart from competitors who might appear greedy and self-centered by comparison.

When the event benefits charity, you may be able to get discounted or free products from some of your suppliers. Spirits distributors often have this discretion. The charity connection may enable you to get a distributor or product manufacturer to co-sponsor the event. If this happens, it will lower your costs and bring more marketing muscle into the event. Local celebrities are more likely to turn out for a charity event, and their presence can help build attendance for the occasion.

Best of all, the charity itself will help promote the event to its members and supporters, which can bring new people in to experience your restaurant.

Where do you start? Well, a savvy GBM practitioner will look for regular guests who can influence a significant amount of business and find out how you can help them help their favorite causes.

For example, let's say that one of your regular patrons is the CEO of a large local company. Ask her what charities are important to her or her company and offer to host a fundraiser for that group. Listen to her suggestions as to how you could best serve the charity, come up with a plan, and let her introduce the idea to the group. In this way, the idea will be presented by an insider, she will enhance her position with the charity, and you will become her ally in the project.

In the process of working with the CEO to set up the fundraiser, you will strengthen the personal relationship she has with your restaurant. This, in turn, may help assure that you get first crack at her company's future function business. In any case, it will tie her closer to you and that can't hurt.

51

Festivals

From the aspect of GBM, festivals provide a natural, logical reason to invite guests to return and to give them something to talk to their friends about. "Come back next week for our Salmon Festival" sounds much better than "Come back on Tuesday because it's slow and we need the business!"

Festivals are special events highlighting a particular cuisine or a food product. They are a great way to break the monotony for staff and guests alike. In addition, they provide a way to experiment with new recipes and take advantage of seasonal products.

Festivals can be run on a specific night (such as a "Thursday is International Night" program) or for a specific period of time, usually a week or two. Festivals that run longer than a month will lose their specialness and might create some confusion in the minds of the market as to what sort of a restaurant you are.

General thoughts on festivals   No matter what sort of festivals you conduct, they must be appropriate for your restaurant. I have a hard time imagining a successful Russian food festival in a pizzeria, for example. However, an Italian restaurant could easily run a festival featuring shellfish.

Festivals should be run often enough to break up the routine but not so frequently that they lose their uniqueness, confuse the market, or become a career in themselves. A two-week festival once a quarter is a realistic goal in most restaurants because it coincides with the change of seasons and does not overwhelm either the staff or the guests.

If the festival is successful, you have the routine down, and the guests are excited, you could consider an every-other-month schedule. But take it slowly and make sure that you do a memorable job with each event. Build on a strong foundation.

Regional/international cuisines   Cuisines of other areas are fertile ground for promotional festivals. The most obvious themes are based on foods from other countries. At the least, these festivals would feature foods, recipes, beers and wines from the selected country.

If you want to get serious about it (and you do!), each international festival could include ethnic background music (perhaps with native performers), costumes and decorations from the country, educational materials about the country, and cultural displays (folk art, posters, photographs, and so forth).

You might invite a chef from the featured country to work with your staff during the festival and/or to prepare a special kick-off dinner for the affair. You might contact the country's embassy or consulate for posters and other support.

You could give away a trip to the country as an incentive for guests to visit you during the festival. To explore this option, make friends with a travel agent (they often have access to discount promotional trips) and see if you can barter with them for prizes. Airlines based in the featured country (like Lufthansa from Germany) may have a deal on a ticket. At the least, they will probably have material you can use to execute the theme.

Remember that the more unusual your approach to the festival, the more special it will be and the more "talking power" it will have on the street.

In addition to ethnic cuisines, regional American cooking can offer powerful promotional possibilities and provide the same potential for authentic recipes, foods, beverages, and cultural support materials.

Here is a partial list of potential regional and international themes to start you thinking about what could work for your restaurant:

New England	Southwest	Northwest
Tex-Mex	California	Gulf Coast
Cajun	Heartland	Santa Fe Trail
Chinese	Brazilian	Middle East
German	Russian	Thai
Indian	Mexican	Moroccan
Italian	Indonesian	Greek
Caribbean	Hungarian	French
Scandinavian	Mediterranean	African

Food product festivals   Product festivals typically coincide with the height of the season for that particular product (a July strawberry festival, for example) when supplies are at their peak, quality is the highest, and prices are at their low points.

That being said, there might be some real talking power in off-season festivals (like a fresh raspberry festival in February) if you can locate a source of the product at a cost you can live with.

Protein products (like lobster) lend themselves to an array of appetizers, soups, salads, and entrees featuring the product. Fruit or vegetable products can be worked into appetizers, soups, salads, side dishes, sauces, and desserts.

Here are a few products that could easily be the focus for a festival:

lobster	turkey	nuts
lamb	salmon	sausage
citrus	melon	strawberry
raspberry	apricot	avocado
artichoke	pheasant	venison
crab	wild game	spinach
zucchini	mushroom	garlic
oyster	tomato	cherry
cheese	shrimp	pumpkin
cranberry	buffalo	apple

52

Customer Loyalty Programs

The premise behind customer loyalty programs, or as I prefer to call them, frequent diner plans (FDPs), is that people tend to do what they are rewarded for. What I most like about the concept is that the airlines have already done the basic consumer education on the idea.

The incentive for implementing an FDP is to encourage repeat patronage, thereby increasing sales volume. The discount structure of the FDP also has the effect of lowering prices for members of the plan, which can be helpful in tourist markets where you want to keep prices up while keeping your operation affordable to the locals. The "insider" appeal of belonging to an FDP also helps members identify more closely with your restaurant, much as they would identify with a private club to which they belong.

Frequent Flyers

Airline frequent flyer plans have done exactly what they were designed to do—they have created consumer loyalty and differentiated a product (airline seats) which would otherwise be a commodity. While they may represent a tiger by the tail for the airlines, they have given passengers a reason to give preference to one carrier over another.

For example, a member of the Delta Sky Miles program would prefer to fly with Delta instead of another carrier of which they were not part of such a program. This may be true even if the other carrier had a slightly lower price on the flight.

Frequent diner plans reward guests for continued loyalty. Since the goal of GBM is simply to get guests back one more time a month, including a frequent diner program in your plans can be extremely effective.

Survey Results

A recent study by American Express made it clear that there is a great deal of interest in keeping guests coming back! Over 2,600 operators responded to a survey on customer loyalty programs and the results were quite interesting.

Of total survey respondents:

- 78% of the respondents consider frequent diners to be customers who dine in their restaurants more than 15 times per year.

- 60% rely on recognizing frequent customers in the restaurant or reviewing the reservation book. Only a small percentage use computers to track them.
- About half (46%) say thank you by offering complimentary appetizers, desserts, or drinks. Over 25% invite loyal customers to special events and parties and 15% send holiday greetings or a gift.
- Approximately 20% have a customer loyalty program in place, while almost as many (17%) are considering starting one.

Of respondents who have a customer loyalty program:

- Half (49%) of the existing programs have been in place for 2–5 years and 34% for one year or less. The oldest program represented in the survey began in 1963.
- Few (less than 10%) charge customers for enrollment.
- Nearly all distribute membership cards of some kind—about 22% as ID and 76% as a punch card to keep track of visits. In 80% of these programs, customers must visit 5–10 times before earning any rewards. Approximately 8% require more than 10 visits and 9% require less than five visits to earn rewards.
- All focus on getting customers back into the restaurant to collect rewards. Over 75% offer discounts and about one-fourth offer complimentary desserts, entrees, or full meals; drinks or bottles of wine. Over 25% have programs for lunch only.

You can see that there are a number of variations on the FDP idea. All are based on rewarding guests for their return patronage, but the mechanics and logistics differ. I group them into three basic types:

Punch cards through which a certain number of visits or a certain level of purchases is required to earn a reward.

Point systems through which each visit or purchase earns points that can be redeemed for various rewards.

Percentage of purchase programs through which the guest earns a reward based on a specified percentage of their purchases.

The following chapters discuss variations on the FDP idea that you can use to reward your guests for their loyalty.

53

Punch Cards

Perhaps the most common sort of frequent diner plan involves punch cards such as the sample included as Figure 53-1. Typically, the cards are issued for free and every time the guest purchases a meal, the card is punched, stamped, or initialed. When guests have purchased a predetermined number of meals (ten seems like the most common number), they receive a free meal. Occasionally, cards are keyed to the dollar value of the purchases.

Advantages

Perhaps the major advantage of punch cards is that they are inexpensive and easy to produce. You can easily do the layout yourself or ask your printer to come up with a design. Be sure to include the details of the offer along with your logo, name, address, and phone number. Pick a stock that will be strong enough to hold

L	L	L	L	L	L	L	L
L	**Your Restaurant** 1234 Main Street • Anytown, USA • (800) 555-1212						L
D	**Buy 10 Lunch Entrees Get 1 Free** **Buy 10 Dinner Entrees Get 1 Free** (One Card Per Customer, One Stamp per Visit)						L
D	D	D	D	D	D	D	D

Figure 53-1

up in the guest's wallet and a color that will be distinctive. You want guests to be reminded of you when they open their wallets.

Punch cards also require a minimum of administration time. The restaurant only has to handle the issue, validation, and redemption of the physical cards. The completed card is essentially a free meal coupon which can be handled as a cash alternative.

Disadvantages

Punch cards have several disadvantages as well. They are prone to abuse since the validation typically is done by hand. It is easy for staff to punch a card several times without anyone knowing it. Systems that require initials and dates can help get around this problem but add to the handling.

Without dates of use, you will not get a patronage history from punch cards. You may know that a guest has been in ten times but you do not know how long it took to accumulate the required number of validations. You cannot tell if the diner's frequency is increasing or decreasing and there is no way to identify guests who have stopped coming in.

Lost or forgotten cards can also be an annoyance. For example, a guest says he forgot his card the last time he was in and you owe him an extra punch. You have no way to know exactly what happened, so it is easy to beat the system. Some operators have addressed this issue by keeping the cards in a box at the restaurant and pulling it when the guest comes in. This has the advantage of letting you know the guest's name and the card is always there, but you lose the reminder value of having your card in the diner's wallet.

Watch Your Offer

Whatever your offer, be sensitive to how realistic it will seem to the guest. After all, the purpose of the program is to encourage repeat patronage, not to discourage it. If the number of purchases required seems intimidating ("It will take me forever to eat there fifteen times") the card loses its incentive value. When in doubt, less is more because everyone likes instant gratification.

Case Studies

The most generous punch card program I have heard of is used by Pearson House in West Milton, Ohio. They have a "Diner Card" with rows of dollar amounts ($1, $2, and $3) totaling $100. After each meal, the dollar amount spent is punched on the card. For each completely punched card, customers receive two free meals of their choice, plus beverage (maximum retail value is $32). Since 1992, over 24,000 cards have been issued; 7,000 have been redeemed (one customer has redeemed 120!).

The Park Cafe and 8th Street Grill in Minneapolis also uses punch cards and designates Mondays as "double punch" days.

I recently received the following e-mail message from Jeff Benporath in South Africa regarding his company's approach to an FDP which is a variation on the punch card idea. He wrote, "We run (at present) the largest pub chain in South Africa named 'Kegs'. They are traditional English pubs and we have what we call the 'Keg Green Card' (don't get confused with the USA green card—our corporate color is green!). We sell it for R35.00 and it offers diners R375 worth of meals 'on the house'. A quick calculation will show that 15 meals of R25 equals R375. (Note: R25 means 25 Rand, the South African unit of currency.)

"The way it operates is that the cheaper of the two main meals (up to a value of R25) gets deducted from the bill. In addition to this, if you are from another province (a province is the same as a state), we will buy you the first round of drinks. The card is great. Not only do guests fill in their name and address (allowing us to send them our 'Keg Times' via mail—our guest database sits at 10,000 names thanks to this), but it also encourages them to go to a Keg before frequenting one of the numerous other restaurants in the area. Verdict . . . it surely works. CHEERS!"

54

Point Systems

Point systems operate by assigning points to the cardholder's account based on the dollar value of purchases made in the restaurant. Typically each dollar spent on food and beverage earns one point. Tax and tip are not normally included in the point total since they do not represent income to the operator. The points accumulate and can be redeemed for merchandise at different award levels.

You can make arrangements with local merchants to trade meals for merchandise. The way this would work is that if a cycle shop provides a $600 bicycle that can be used as an award, they receive $600 in meal credits at the restaurant. The cycle effectively "buys" the meal credits for the wholesale cost of the bicycle and the restaurant obtains the bike for the cost of the meals provided.

Advantages

A program such as this provides more options for the members of the plan than if the points could be used only for meals. Relationships built with vendors as part of a program like this can result in long-term business and mutual promotional activities.

Disadvantages

The logistics of a point system are more complicated than other frequent diner programs. You have to negotiate with vendors for products and it is difficult to know exactly what prizes people will want. If everyone wants a bicycle, for example, how long will it be before the cycle shop has all the meal credits it can use and asks you to start paying cash?

Case Studies

The 20-unit California Restaurant Group (CRG) has 200,000 members in their Cafe Club Awards Program, a point-based FDP, the details of which are included in Figure 54-1. Points accumulate at the rate of one per dollar spent and can be redeemed for merchandise, meals, or travel. Members are credited with 100 points just for joining and may start redeeming points as soon as they have reached the 250 point level. Because of their volume, CRG can negotiate joint marketing arrangements with various sponsors that enable the company to obtain merchandise under favorable terms.

Pamela Hartnett, the Cafe Club program administrator, admits that the merchandise aspect of their program is harder to manage but feels that the variety helps keep members more interested than could be accomplished with meal rewards alone. She also cautions

---

CAFE CLUB TERMS AND CONDITIONS

The Cafe Club Card is not a credit card and is not valid for purchases. By accepting receipt of the Cafe Club Card issued by California Restaurant Group, for use by the person named thereon, "Cardholder" agrees as follows:

1. Cardholder shall be bound by all of the terms and conditions contained herein, on the Cafe Club Card, on the Cafe Club Awards Program notifications, and by all applicable laws. All interpretations of Program Terms and Conditions shall be at the sole discretion of California Restaurant Group. Federal and state tax liabilities shall be the responsibility of the Cardholder.

2. Points will be credited to the Cardholder's account for amounts spent by the Cardholder dining at California Restaurant Group restaurants. Members shall be entitled to point credit only upon presentation of their membership card at the time of meal payment. Points are not awarded for payments made with Cafe Club Dining Award certificates, restaurant gift certificates, or in conjunction with other dining discounts or promotions. Cardholder shall be entitled to credit based on a point system whereby one (1) point for every dollar spent, exclusive of gratuity, will be credited to Cardholder's account. Liquor control laws in some states may prohibit point credit for alcoholic beverage purchases.

3. Cardholder shall receive a Cafe Club Awards Program statement on a periodic basis, indicating points accrued. Statements are mailed only to those members with account activity within the six (6) months prior to statement publication. Members are responsible for notifying the Cafe Club of address changes. California Restaurant Group is not responsible for delayed or undeliverable mail.

4. Cafe Club cards, memberships and accrued points do not constitute the property of the Cardholder and are not transferable. However, accrued points and Award certificates may be redeemed by either party listed on joint memberships. Illegal, fraudulent or other unauthorized use of the Cafe Club card, vouchers and certificates, or any other activity inconsistent with the Program Terms and Conditions shall result in termination of Cardholder's membership and forfeiture of accrued points.

5. California Restaurant Group reserves the right to modify the Program terms, conditions, reward structure and awards, or to terminate the program at any time without advance notice.

6. California Restaurant Group is not responsible for interpretation by its employees of Program procedure, terms and conditions. In the event of any conflict, this agreement (as modified) and/or the most recent Cafe Club Awards Program notification(s) shall control.

7. California Restaurant Group employees and their families are not eligible for Cafe Club membership.

Figure 54-1

operators not to undertake an FDP unless they are prepared to sustain it. Members love the benefits, she says, and to discontinue or seriously cut back an FDP program once it has a following may actually create resentment toward the restaurant.

The Levy Restaurants in Chicago has a program called "Levy Preferred" that is a hybrid between a percentage and a point program. Once guests sign up (there is no charge), they receive one point for each dollar they spend on food and beverage in any of Levy's five participating Chicago restaurants. Every time a guest spends $250, the guest receives a $25 gift certificate. Certificates can be redeemed in any of the participating restaurants or accumulated for premium awards like trips.

55

Percentage of Purchase Plans

A percentage of purchase format is closest to the airline frequent flyer programs that form the basis for the FDP idea.

In a percentage-based FDP, members receive a rebate on their purchases. The credit is typically about 10% of everything they purchase in the restaurant, including catering services. Usually the credits accumulate until they reach a predetermined total, at which point a gift certificate is issued.

This approach avoids discounting your basic prices. In other words, guests do not pay $8.95 for a $9.95 entree tonight. They pay full price tonight and get a $1 credit for a future meal. Structuring the plan this way gives guests a reason to return to the restaurant next month, developing a habit that can only work to your advantage. It also provides for more immediate gratification than most other FDP approaches.

Mechanics of a Percentage Plan

You may be wondering what to expect if you actually implement a percentage-based FDP. I cannot make any promises, but I will share some statistics developed by Bob Henslee of Frequency Systems in Jupiter, Florida. Bob's company administers percentage-based FDPs for thousands of clients and he reports the following.

First of all, he says that for every million dollars in gross sales, you can expect to have about 1,000 members signed up for your FDP. These members will tend to distribute themselves into three distinct groups:

15% heavy hitters (four or more visits a month)

50% core patrons (2–3 visits a month)

35% occasional users (less than two visits per month)

Not only are these groups identifiable, each requires a different marketing approach.

Heavy Hitters

These are the regulars whom everybody knows by name. Your goal here is simply retention—you want to keep their loyalty. Marketing activities with the heavy hitters consist of personal gestures to tie them more closely to the restaurant. This could take the form of free tickets to sporting events, perhaps with limo transportation. You might want to acknowledge major events in their lives (like a new baby, a new house, and so forth) with a card or small gift. Even something as simple as a personal phone call on the member's birthday will go a long way to keeping these valuable guests on your side.

The heavy hitters should also be tapped for a focus group from time to time. Gather a group of ten or so, buy them lunch, and solicit their suggestions as to how to make the restaurant better and more responsive. Their perspective is more objective than yours and everybody will gain from the experience.

Core Patrons

Your goal with the core group is to increase frequency and encourage referrals. This can be done through special offers, many of which are suggested elsewhere in this book. Special offers can also include double FDP points on a particular night or "two-fer" deals for these patrons only.

Bob's experience is that a 2% increase in core group activity translates into a 10% increase in sales! This figure is pretty impressive, but a 2% increase may seem difficult to achieve. Fortunately, one of the potent benefits of mailing to the FDP list is that the response on mailings is significant. Bob says that a 20–40% return on direct mail offers is typical. He even told of an offer mailed out by Leverock Seafood Restaurants in Florida that generated an incredible 52% response! They offered double points during the month of December and saw a triple-digit increase in sales!

How did *your* last mailing do?

Occasional Users

This group is essentially trial rejecters. They tried your restaurant and didn't like the experience enough to make you a habit. You still want to encourage frequency from this group, but they are most valuable as a source of research. After all, you know who they are and they know why they have not been back. They have a wealth of insights into how to make your operation more user-friendly and can help you pinpoint the breakdowns that are costing you business every day.

The occasional users should also be recruited for focus groups following the process outlined above. Most of these folks will be delighted that you asked for—and listened to—their opinions. Your caring might also jump-start their renewed patronage!

MIAs

Logging the activity of the FDP members will help you flag patrons who are missing in action. These are folks who used to come in regularly and who have broken their pattern or have not been seen for awhile. Bob's experience is that you can recover 87% of these folks just by calling to find out what happened. Usually it is some personal lapse like not being acknowledged promptly or being treated with indifference.

Listen to what these guests have to say and offer a gift certificate for a second chance to show them that you can do a better job than they experienced the last time. They will be impressed that you noticed their absence, appreciate the personal concern, and usually start coming in again. Without an FDP to collect this data, you would not be able to identify MIAs at all and you would just lose them forever.

For information on program administrators such as Frequency Systems and The Customer Connection, see "Resources" on page 203.

Cards

Members of the FDP receive a plastic "credit card." Personally, I question whether flimsy cardboard cards have the "wallet appeal" you need to have the plan taken seriously. These cards can be printed with any copy you want and can be as simple or as elaborate as you like. Cost is quite reasonable. (Several sources for these cards are listed in the "Resources" section on page 203.)

The fastest way to handle the logistics is to buy cards pre-embossed with a 5-digit number. If you then design the cards with a signature panel on the front, you have a relatively personalized card that you can issue on the spot. The number can also be pre-encoded on a magnetic stripe on the back of the card for electronic transaction capture.

You can also have the member's name embossed much like conventional credit cards. This approach creates modest increases in card costs and issuing time. It also adds more handling. It does create a more personal, and therefore potentially more valuable, card with a higher perceived value to the guest. If you wish, all the logistics of card preparation and issuing can be handled by a third party. (See the "Resources" section on page 203.)

If you want to start simply, you could use the prenumbered cards until you have verified that the FDP is going to be a big hit, then move into personalized cards.

Membership Fees

FDP cards can carry a fee of up to $25.00, although few operators actually levy the charge. The fee creates value for the card . . . and you can always waive the charge as a courtesy gesture. You can also credit a new member's account with the amount of the fee or donate the fee to a local charity. Regardless, you may want to "prime the pump" by crediting some money to the new member's account for use next month. (Many airlines give new members a 5,000-mile credit when they sign up.)

Data Capture

FDP purchases can be captured electronically using the mag stripe or manually by running a regular charge voucher using the embossed numbers on the FDP card. These slips can be collected and manually sorted at the end of the month.

It is difficult to stay current on all the electronic options as the market changes every day. If you are considering a new Point-of-Sale (POS) system, ask if they have software that will facilitate record-keeping for an FDP.

For example, Squirrel Systems has a club package that can be added to their basic POS system. Diners actually pay for their meals by conventional means, but the software allows you to "charge" frequent diners' purchases to members' "accounts" and accumulate the purchases automatically. The Squirrel club package will also provide access to a database on each member when the account number is entered.

Some companies are marketing software packages for your existing back office computer. These programs will enable you to track the activity in your frequent diner program and develop statistical reports. (See "Resources" on page 203 for more information.)

Advantages

The most obvious advantage to the FDP member is the discount on purchases. You might offer FDP members preferred reservations. While members may not realize it, they are also likely to receive an improved level of service because the restaurant staff is more apt to know their names and their personal preferences.

The most obvious advantage to the operator is increased repeat business. This results from a higher frequency of individual patronage plus the incentive for increased use of other restaurant services such as catering. The FDP files provide a far more detailed database than most operators would be able to generate without the plan. Usage data will also allow you to track frequency of repeat patrons, check averages, and related stats.

I think FDPs, particularly percentage-based plans, are one of the most cost-effective ways to reward guests for doing what you want them to do—return regularly to your restaurant! Here are a few ways that operators around the country are using the FDP idea.

Case Studies

Warren's Lobster House in Kittery, Maine has had a percentage-based FDP since 1991. Every time a guest's spending totals $100, they receive a $10 gift certificate for a future visit to the restaurant. The total upon which the percentage is based includes actual cash (or credit card) expenditures for food and beverage purchases. The card itself is a plastic "credit card" with a magnetic strip. The card is issued without a fee and personalized with the guest's name. Warren's FDP members can make priority reservations during the busy summer season and receive a monthly newsletter. The card must be used twice a year to stay active.

TGI Friday's operates a plan called "Frequent Fridays™" that is administered by The Customer Connection. Friday's awards ten points for each dollar spent with 5,750 points earning a $15 dining certificate. For those of you who are keen on the details of such a plan, the "small print" from the Friday's brochure is included in

Figure 55-1. This information is provided only as an example, not necessarily as a model.

On a (slightly) contrary note, Randy Rayburn of Sunset Grill in Nashville has elected not to establish a frequent diner plan. His business has been building steadily because of an active GBM program and a passionate commitment to guest delight. He sees no need for an FDP until his sales growth starts to flatten out. This reinforces the notion that there is no reason to discount anything you can sell just as well at full price.

LEGAL GOBBLEDYGOOK YOU CAN READ
IF YOU'RE REALLY, REALLY BORED

1. Offer good at participating T.G.I. Friday's® Front Row® Sports Grill and Italianni's® restaurants.

2. No purchase is necessary to get a Frequent Friday's™ Card. But purchase is required to earn points.

3. To earn points, you, the member, must present your card at the time of purchase.

4. You'll be awarded (10) base points for every $1 purchased. Some restrictions on alcohol purchases may apply. A really cool-looking Frequent Friday's™ receipt will serve as confirmation that the points were credited to your account.

5. Points may be earned only by the Frequent Friday's™ card holder who pays the check. Also, points earned or redeemed don't apply towards gratuity. Frequent Friday's™ points will not be issued on the purchase of gift certificates. Points will be awarded upon gift certificate redemption.

6. Because we're really nice, (500) bonus points will be automatically added to each new membership. These points will appear on member's point balance within three days of membership activation.

7. Check out your Frequent Friday's™ receipt, because it may have a printed "Bonus Point Offer." This allows you to earn "a stated multiple of points on a future purchase made within the stated redemption period." In other words, you'll get lots of chances to earn beaucoup bonus points. Whee!

8. Hi mom!

9. Here's a long one: to redeem points for an award, you should notify a server that you want to redeem your points and what award you want to get. After you present your card to your server, the point balance will be electronically confirmed and deducted from your balance. An award certificate will be printed and must be exchanged for the selected prize. Travel awards require advance notice. Please call 1-800-xxx-xxxx for further details. Airline awards apply to round trip travel within the contiguous US. Travel awards will be non-refundable, may require a Saturday night stay and some blackout dates may apply. Cruise award doesn't include airfare.

10. Awards may vary by store.

11. T.G.I. Friday's Inc., at its sole discretion, can modify the program awards or substitute awards of a comparable value without notice.

12. T.G.I. Friday's Inc. reserves the right to discontinue this program at any time. In the event that this program is discontinued, members will be allowed to redeem all points earned.

13. OK, T.G.I. Friday's Inc. also reserves the right to discontinue membership privileges and void a member's point balance if any unauthorized points are earned or redeemed.

14. At Friday's Front Row® Sports Grill, points will not be awarded on ticket and game purchases and room rentals.

15. Certain states may have additional restrictions.

16. Hey, Frequent Friday's™ points expire five years following the last day of the year in which they are issued. T.G.I. Friday's Inc. also reserves the right to discontinue membership privileges and/or void a member's point balance, if that member's account has shown no activity over a period of not less than eighteen months.

17. Employees of T.G.I. Friday's Inc., its franchisees, affiliates, subsidiaries, and immediate families of each are not eligible.

**For participating locations or for Official Rules and Conditions
call Frequent Friday's™ customer service at 1-800-xxx-xxxx**

Figure 55-1

A Modest Proposal

As a final note many companies are hard-pressed to afford the holiday parties that can be such a positive morale factor. If you have function facilities and an FDP, why not make an offer that the businesses in your market area will find it hard to refuse? Offer to establish a corporate account and provide FDP cards to all the business's employees. Whenever anyone from the company dines with you, the points accumulate for a end-of-the-year bash. In this way, if the group generated $30,000 in sales for you by November, they would have $3,000 to put toward a Christmas party at your restaurant!

Build Personal Connection

56

It's about People, Stupid!

Foodservice is a business based on personal connection. If you can successfully establish that connection, it will change the way your restaurant is regarded in the minds of your guests. Personal connection will move you from the category of being just another eating place to the status of being a friend of the family.

Personal connection is an integral part of GBM because it is based on increasing frequency from your existing patrons and *guests come back because they want to*. If you accept the premise that people prefer to be treated as individuals rather than indifferently, the restaurant that can create the closest personal connection is apt to be the restaurant most frequently patronized.

Personal connection comes when I, as the operator, take good care of you as the guest . . . because it is YOU. It is more likely to develop from actions taken in response to individual situations rather than from actions dictated by some sort of blanket corporate policy (although corporate policy may be required to give staff members authority to take individual action).

Personal connection comes from giving guests the benefit of the doubt, from earning their trust and from recognizing, even celebrating, their individuality and personal quirks.

The Answer Is "Yes"

Personal connection comes from listening—really listening—to guests and finding ways to say "yes" rather than ways to say "no." It is an attitude that "Coach" Don Smith would describe as, "The answer is yes. What's the question?"

Interestingly, getting the staff to say "yes" starts with the attitude and actions of management. Write this down: *Your staff will treat your guests the same way you treat your staff.*

What they see is what you will get. Your behavior toward your crew in the daily course of business provides the model for how your staff will behave when a guest makes a "weird request" or does something they were not "supposed to" have done.

57

Presence

The secret to personal connection and creating impact with others is presence. Simply put, presence is a state of mind that is free from distraction. Your level of presence is the extent to which your mind is not occupied with thoughts unrelated to the project at hand.

Here are a few examples of what I mean. Have you ever been talking to someone who was listening to you . . . and then suddenly they *weren't* listening to you? They may even have been looking at you and nodding their heads as you spoke, but didn't you know when their attention was elsewhere?

How about this: Have you talked with someone on the phone while they were doing something else at the same time? Even though you couldn't see them, hasn't it been obvious when you did not have their total attention? These are both instances of distraction or low presence.

Now recall your experience of what it feels like to talk to someone who was not really listening to you. If you are like most people, you probably find that distracted behavior to be rude at best and angering at worst.

Distractions

A distracted state of mind creates irritation in other people. You know how incredibly annoying it can be to talk with someone whose mind has wandered. Yet we do the same thing to people constantly because we have accepted the notion that the way to be efficient and get more done is to do several tasks at once. In fact, effectiveness comes from just the opposite approach.

Here is a typical scene in foodservice: you have the phone in one ear while you are working on the schedule and trying to handle a staff member's question at the same time! Sound familiar? My guess is that neither the person on the other end of the phone, nor the schedule, nor your staff member got the quality of attention they really needed. In all likelihood you probably had to go back to one or all of these "projects" for clarification, to correct mistakes, or to make another try at resolving "problems" that could easily have been avoided if you were not so distracted the first time.

Lessons from Life

Imagine a two year-old is looking for attention and you are busy. As they tug on your pants leg you say "Later, kid, I'm busy" without looking up from your work. Do they respond with "Oh sure, Daddy, I understand?" Not a chance!

To take care of a two-year-old you have to drop what you are doing, get down eyeball to eyeball, and give the child your undivided attention for about five seconds. If you do this, you will buy yourself some time. You may get a few minutes and you may get an hour, but if children don't get your complete attention, they will pull on you for the rest of their natural lives!

It is no different if they are 22 or 62. Mostly what people want to know is that you "got it"—that whatever they had to say actually got through to you, and this cannot happen if you are distracted. The only difference between dealing with children and adults is that kids are more honest—they will not pretend that they have your attention if your mind is wandering. Adults are usually more polite but no less observant.

Presence and Productivity

The truth is that you can really only concentrate on one thing at a time anyway. When you are talking with another person, there is nothing you can do at that same moment about finishing the schedule (or your food cost, your sick child, or your vacation, etc.). If your mind is occupied with extraneous thoughts, your attention is not fully with the person in front of you. Even if they do not call you on it, they will notice. If the interaction is with your staff, they will keep coming back again and again trying to get through to you. If the interaction is with your guests, they may never come back.

As with children, you can handle a situation in 5 seconds or 5 hours—the only difference is your level of presence when you do it. So the secret to productivity is to handle things exactly the way you would with a child. Drop distractions, focus your attention, handle one item at a time, and move on to the next project. Presence (lack of distraction) will enable you to more accurately assess the situation and quickly deal with it in a more effective way.

Presence and Service

In my service staff seminars, I point out that the reason guests leave a tip of 10% or 30% depends in large measure on the level of personal connection servers create with their guests. Presence increases the personal connection between people. In fact, without presence, there is no personal connection at all.

Last week I watched one server increase his tips from 12% one night to over 25% the next night by doing nothing more than keeping his head clear when he was at the table. A pizzeria manager told me that over half of his "people problems" seemed to disappear when he started becoming aware of (and dropping) distracting thoughts. In both cases, I asked them what they were doing differently. Both persons replied, "I am just trying to be with people when I am with people."

When your guests have a complaint or when members of your staff have a question, what they want most is to feel that you really *heard* what they had to say. Most people do not expect you to resolve their every concern on the spot, but they want to sense that what they had to say was important to you.

Presence and State of Mind

Just as a distracted state of mind creates irritation, presence makes people feel more positive. The feeling of being important is really a function of presence. What do you think the impact of presence (or lack of it) might be on how well-served your guests feel in the restaurant? What do you think the impact of presence (or lack of it) might be on how much your staff feels that you care for them?

You convey your level of caring by your level of presence. If you are distracted, people do not feel listened to and will continue to voice their concerns until either they know that you got the message or they give up on you. (By the way, when they give up on you, they will probably leave for a competitor . . . or for another job!)

If you have ever worked for someone who did not listen, you know the feeling of being ignored. You can't tell someone who does not listen that they do not listen because, well, they do not listen! Most people who do not listen really think that they do. Your challenge is to be sure that you are not guilty of the same sin when someone needs your attention.

A Natural State

Presence is not something unnatural—all of us are born with high presence. Little babies have high presence because their heads aren't yet cluttered with thoughts—they only know how to deal with what is right in front of them at the moment.

This sounds too simple, but look at what happens when you bring a newborn baby into a room. Everyone's attention shifts to the baby. People start to smile and forget about their own problems for a few minutes. The baby is not *doing* anything—just being there— yet everyone around feels a little better.

This demonstrates the power presence has to make others feel more positive. High presence is our birthright, but it is also something we can easily lose sight of as the pace of business speeds up, our lives become increasingly complex, and we take on more "responsibilities".

Staying on Track

Now it is unrealistic to think that you can always operate without distractions, but you can at least start to be aware of distracting thoughts when they begin to clutter your mind. One way to tell is that this is happening when people you are talking with start to get restless or when you see a glazed look in their eyes. When your attention wanders, so will theirs. Another clue is that you will have a hard time "connecting" with others.

The good news is that simply becoming aware of the fact that you are distracted will start to put you back on track. When you notice that you are becoming distracted, just gently let go of whatever stray thoughts are in your head and bring your attention back to the task at hand. Your increased presence will make your audience feel better served and bring more impact to your message.

Here are a few "homework" exercises that can help you increase your presence:

✔ Notice how often you are distracted at work and at home.
✔ Notice how you automatically start the process of self-correction toward greater presence just by becoming aware of being distracted.

Presence is not something you *do*, it is a state that you are either in or not in. Becoming more sensitive to those clues that warn you that your attention is wandering will help make you a natural expert with people, reduce your level of stress, and greatly increase your enjoyment of life both on and off the job.

58

Guest Recognition

I am sure you all appreciate your guests. After all, where would you be without them? But what do you do to let them know how important they are to you? What do you do to make them feel more important and draw them closer to your restaurant? What do you do to massage their egos and elevate them in the eyes of their peers?

Does that sound like a tall order? It is easier to do than you may imagine. The following examples illustrate a few approaches that have worked for other operators. Perhaps you will find an idea or two that you can adapt.

Patron Profiles in the Newsletter

Do you publish a newsletter that goes to your guests? Along with the recipe of the month, the news of your current promotion and the biography of the waitress just completing her tenth year with you, why not include a profile of one of your regular patrons? After all, the restaurant exists for the good of the guests, doesn't it?

How can you get this information? Ask!

Imagine the stroke to someone's sense of importance to be interviewed for a feature article. If you ask around the restaurant, you probably have someone with journalism experience who can conduct the interview (although I suggest that the manager or owner still be involved for the prestige it will lend to the process).

Wall of Fame

The wall of fame is a way to recognize your regulars, usually by mounting their photo or their caricature on the wall of the restaurant. If you elect to recognize someone this way, a few words of caution:

1. **Establish selection criteria.** There has to be some objective standard that determines whether someone is eligible for enshrinement on your wall of fame. If it just happens at the whim of the manager or someone on the staff, it becomes a game of favorites and has no importance to those outside the inner circle. It could even cause resentment.
2. **Don't surprise anyone.** Be sure you have permission before you consign people to immortality. If people prefer not to have their picture posted, respect their wishes. No matter how curious you might be, do not pry into their reasons. If you post

their picture against their wishes, you work against the goal of the honor, which is to make people feel closer to your operation.

3. **Make it an event.** To have others regard enshrinement as truly an honor, you must treat it as such. Adding someone to the wall can follow a traditional ceremony. Since you get to establish the tradition in the first place, give it some thought. Come up with something that will be fun, memorable, not (too) embarrassing to the participants, and that will bring you in a little money!

   At the least, the honoree should invite friends to witness the event. Schedule the enshrinement on a night when business would otherwise be slow. You can use the business and there will be less distractions to pull your attention away from the person being honored.

   The unveiling of the picture should be preceded by a short testimonial (serious or otherwise) about the person being honored and what was done to merit the honor being bestowed. Their picture, whether it is a photo or a caricature, should be professionally done and presented in a frame of appropriate quality.

4. **Hold a ceremony.** Enshrinement is even more powerful if there is a little ceremony that goes along with the honor. In many cases it will be silly or humorous—something like having the honoree chug a beer, rub tuna fish on his tummy, and buy a round for the house! Just so things aren't too one-sided, you might want to make a contribution to the honoree's charity of choice. Who knows? Just use your imagination and you will be fine.

   The ceremony is part of what will give the honor its meaning. From the aspect of GBM, the enshrinement becomes a reason to invite all your other guests to come back in to witness the ceremony. Take photos. Give one set to the honoree and post a second set for those who could not attend.

Outstanding Customer Plaque

There are other ways to recognize guests besides posting pictures. The Steak Joint, in Oklahoma City, hangs an "Outstanding Customer" plaque in the dining room which, after two years, has

390 names on it. Ed Khalil, the owner, says that guests love pointing out their names to their friends.

Customer Awards

David Duthie, owner of The Yellow Brick Toad in Lambertville, New Jersey, does a superb job of guest recognition. Every August he holds an award dinner for his regulars, the highlight of which is the announcement of his "Patron of the Year."

In addition to the annual honor, he also gives out other awards. The Toad is an active supporter of local charities, so David enlists his guests to volunteer their help with a variety of community activities over the course of a year. At the annual banquet he gives out "Being There" awards to those people who helped by being there when they were needed.

Personalized Menu Items

A great way to tie guests to your restaurant is to name a menu item after them. I am sure you have regular guests who always request some special concoction when they come in. If you think it would fly with your other guests, why not name the item after the originator and add it to your regular menu. It will have "talking power" and help the guest identify more closely with the restaurant.

Items like this can easily become signature items for you. In my college days at Cornell during the early 1960s, THE place to hang out in Ithaca was Obie's Diner, a classic railroad-car-type of place with ten seats at the counter and two tables. Obie's was famous for the Bo-Burger, a combination allegedly devised in the early 1950s for Bo Roberson, Cornell's first (and perhaps only?) consensus All-America football player. It consisted of a hamburger with grilled diced onions, a fried egg with a broken yolk, and melted cheese. Bo-burgers were very good to Obie, who sold enough of them to buy a new Cadillac each year and spend every July and August in Spain!

Who knows what incredible items are lurking in the imaginations of your guests?

At Crisis Hopkins, my San Francisco restaurant, we solicited our guests for their favorite recipes. The best ones ran as weekly specials, with appropriate credit given to the contributor, of course! The person who provided the recipe received dinner for four any month that their item appeared on the menu. The result was that we had a huge research department (made up of our guests) who were making regular contributions to what they increasingly came to think of as *their* restaurant. In the process, we discovered a number of great items, several of which became regular features on our menu.

A final example of the power of tying guests into the menu is also from the Bay Area.

There was a neighborhood restaurant/bar near my apartment that seemed to have a new owner every year for as long as I lived there. Most owners seemed intent on carving out a place in the overall San Francisco restaurant market, but they all died trying.

Finally, a group bought the place and after the obligatory name change and interior freshening, went strictly after business from the immediate neighborhood. To create the local connection, they named all the menu items after the area residents who suggested them (for example, the Nora Daly sandwich or Fettucini Isaacman). They did a good job with the basics, gave every guest personal treatment, and became a popular local hangout. Interestingly, word of their success got around and it wasn't too long before they became a citywide destination!

Personalized Booths or Seats

Another way to honor a regular patron is to engrave his name on a brass plate and attach it to his favorite booth, table, or bar stool. All the criteria listed for the wall of fame apply to this honor as well. It is up to you to determine what special privileges accompany such an honor, if any.

Along this line, it seems that an increasingly popular way to finance public projects is by selling personalized bricks which are then used to pave walkways and other public areas. Perhaps there is a variation on that idea that could be used to help tie guests more closely to your restaurant.

Guests' Names on Reader Boards

If you have a reader board, you have media at your command. People love to see their names up in lights and you could give them their 15 minutes of fame. You have as much to gain by using your reader board to make your guests feel special as you do by using it to advertise your specials. When guests make a reservation, ask if they are celebrating a special occasion. If so, see if they would mind if you put it on the reader board. You could easily become *the* place in town to celebrate!

59

Get to Know Your Guests

In a business based on personal connection, you have to get personal. This means going beyond the procedural aspects of service and getting good at the human dimension of service. The key to treating your guests as individuals is to start thinking of them as individuals.

It may be wonderful to look at yesterday's business and see that you served 300 dinners when you were expecting to serve 275.

It is an entirely different mind set to look over yesterday's reservation list, credit card receipts, or frequent diner transactions to see that Phyllis and Wilber Young came in to celebrate their 53rd anniversary, Bobette Gordon hosted a luncheon for local meeting planners, or that you handled a special entree request for Dick Gaven.

Statistics are a good way to keep score and see if you are continually beating last year. However, statistics tell you about the past and the past is history. As a successful operator, you want to get a handle on what will assure your success into the future.

In a "people business" like ours, it's about people, stupid!

The two easiest things to learn about people are also the two most powerful—who they are and what they like. Let's examine each of them.

60

Learn and Use Guests' Names

It is true that people love the sound of their own names, but they also love that they are important enough to you that you remember who they are.

Do you have regular patrons—people who come in all the time? Do you know them by name? Probably so. Most owners and managers get pretty serious about recognizing regulars.

If I was just hired as a member of your staff, is there a *system* in place so that I would quickly start to know who these important people are, or do you leave it to chance?

Shari's, a regional coffee shop chain based in the Pacific Northwest, makes learning and knowing guests' names a part of their culture. Servers who learn the names of 100 regulars get their names engraved on a plaque on the restaurant wall. There are servers in the Shari's organization who know the names of 1,400 regular guests! Do you think patrons get the idea that they are important?

So how can you get to know patrons' names in the first place?

If you take reservations, you can certainly get names from the reservation list. If you have a frequent diner program, you will have the name of the card holder if you ask for their FDP number. At the least, ask people! Your greeters can easily ask for guests' names when they first come in, even if they will be seated immediately. If it is friendly interest and not an interrogation, you should have no problem.

A brief note at the front desk linking name and table number makes it possible for anyone in the organization to know the name of the guest on Table 17. Many managers carry around a clipboard with the names and table numbers on it. (Managers can always carry a clipboard and nobody will think a thing about it. Having the guest information in writing works well for those of us with short memories!)

The next step in any system is a way to get the guest name information from the greeter to the server at the table. Regas Restaurant in Knoxville, Tennessee uses a seating card for this purpose. When guests check in with the greeter, she writes their name on a small tent card. When the party is seated, the card goes on the table so that the waiter or waitress can address the guest by name. The seating card stays on the table throughout the meal and also serves as a comment card.

Writing the guests' name on the back of the check is another way to get the information out there. If the greeter is the control point on guest checks, she could note this information when the guest checks in. If the server has her own checks, she could jot the name on the check when she finds out who the guest is.

Keeping the guests' names continually in front of servers accomplishes three important things:

- They can use the guests' names more frequently.
- They come to associate the name with the face, making it easier to remember the person's name the next time they see him or her.
- They are continually reminded that they are providing service to real people with real lives, not just "the party of three on Table 12."

However you do it, have a conscious, consistent system to get the information from the guest to the server and be sure that the information is being used.

People do what they are rewarded for. If you want your staff to learn and use the names of regulars, reward that behavior. For example, ask a server the name of the guests at one of his tables. If he gets it right (check your clipboard if you are not sure!), slip him a dollar bill or give him a "bonus buck" in script that he can use for a future meal in the restaurant. You could do the same every time you hear a server address a guest by name.

As with any behavior-shaping activity, make a game of it. Do it often enough that everyone knows that you are serious about it and be sure that every server has the experience of winning. Once you are regularly seeing the behavior you want (i.e., they know and use the guests' names), reward them on a random basis. It will keep them interested in the game.

A word of warning: using a guest's name only counts if you use it with respect. This means that you utter their name with the same caring that they would use, usually accompanied with eye contact and a smile.

No matter how casual your restaurant is, it is disrespectful to address guests by their first names until and unless they ask you to do it. This is particularly true with seniors. You will never lose points by being too polite.

The more often you use the guest's name, the easier it will be to remember. The more you use the guest's name, the more often you are likely to see the guest.

61

Remember Guests' Likes and Dislikes

Personal connection comes from taking care of each guest as a unique individual with distinctive needs and wants. This means that not all guests are treated exactly the same.

The golden rule does not apply. Treating guests the way *you* want to be treated will not automatically assure success. You have to treat people the way *they* want to be treated if you want them to feel personally served. How can you treat people the way they want to be treated unless you notice what they need, ask how they want things, and remember what they tell you?

My wife has sensitive teeth, so she prefers her water without ice. This does not seem like anything too complicated, but the simple task of keeping her water glass filled often seems like a meal-long battle! Bussers invariably bring a glass of ice water to her and she has to request a replacement without ice. It is disturbing to see how often bussers are upset by this simple request. It is even more disturbing when they continue to refill her water glass and dump ice into it!

Hello! Was anybody paying attention? Does anybody care?

A world-class restaurant would only need to be told once and they would remember it the next time we came in to dine! When a restaurant remembers, imagine how much more pleasant the dining experience is. When a restaurant remembers, imagine how important the guest feels! All it takes to do this is the desire and a system to support it.

The Rattlesnake Club in Detroit makes a biography card on their regular guests. The cards include all the information the restaurant knows about each guest's needs, inclinations, patterns, and desires. If they have a seating preference, are allergic to certain foods, or have a pet peeve, it is on the card.

After checking the night's reservations, the staff reviews the cards of the guests who will be joining them so that they will have all the personal information fresh in their minds when the guests arrive.

How much do *you* know about your regulars and how is that information made available within the organization? Some POS systems have the capability for an online guest database and I suspect this will become increasingly easy to do. You might find that your system can already handle this feature. It just has to be important enough to you to ask your vendor about it.

62

Personal Information

Being careful not to invade someone's privacy, there is other information you could gather on people who are important to you. What are their personal interests (sports, charities, travel, and the like)? What are their children's names and interests? Are they going on vacation soon? If so, where are they headed?

If you kept a card on each of your regulars, you could make it a game for servers to see if they could add one more thing to the card every time the guest came in. Imagine the caring it would show if the following scene played out in your restaurant: In March regular guests mentioned that they were excited about the Caribbean cruise they were taking in April and it was noted on their card. When they came back to dine in May, the server asks them how they enjoyed their cruise!

What if the server inquired how their daughter Sarah was enjoying soccer this year? It does not matter that a server did not have this information committed to memory and picked up her cue from a 5×7 index card. The fact that the restaurant cares enough to keep track of this information at all speaks volumes and people notice.

Not everyone wants others to know about their personal life, but if you truly enter every encounter with a guest as a unique moment in time with a unique individual, you can easily pick up on their reticence and note it in their file for future reference!

63

"Clubs"

People like to be able to do things that other people cannot do. When you make that possible through establishing a "club" with special privileges for members, you give guests a reason to come back more often, and that is the basis of GBM.

You can make a club out of almost anything. All you need is a premise and a benefit. There are various types of "clubs" that you can use to your advantage. Here are just a few.

Mug Club

Do you sell draft beer? Start a mug club!

Here is the way it works: Members of your mug club receive a personalized beer mug that is kept for them behind the bar. Whenever they come in, they drink from their own mugs and receive a special deal. For example, if you sell a 12-ounce glass of draft beer for $2, the mugs for club members might be 14–16 ounces for the same price.

After attending one of my seminars a few years ago, Jim Casey implemented a mug club at his Casey's East Restaurant in Troy, New York. It costs $4 to join his club (which pays for the mug and your first beer) after which club members can refill their mugs for 25% less than an equal-sized pour would cost for non-members.

When he first started the idea, Jim figured that one or two dozen people might take him up on it. Mug club membership has risen to over 100 in 3 years and continues to grow. The camaraderie among the members helps keep his bar full and Jim has noticed that his regulars have become a lot more regular since the program went into effect.

Mug clubs do not have to be limited to beer. You could adapt the same idea to work with breakfast by finding a really great-looking coffee mug that can be personalized and a deal to make it interesting to "members." You could establish a wine club where members receive a personalized crystal wine glass, the better to (frequently) explore the finer wines from your cellar.

Regardless of their form, the premises behind mug clubs and their kind are similar:

1. The mugs, glasses, cups, or whatever remain at the restaurant, typically on display, so the members have to return to the property to use them.
2. The appearance of the vessel is so distinctive that it is obvious to the other guests in the room when it is being used, making the user (member) feel privileged.
3. The container is personalized with the name of the member and (usually) the logo of the restaurant, the closer to tie the two together.
4. The club member receives a deal—usually either a lower price or more product at the same price—that is not available to nonmembers.

Oyster Club

Do you have an oyster bar? Start a club! Mark Valente, owner of Marc's restaurant in Wheatridge, Colorado, instituted his "200 Oyster Club" several years ago. To become a member, guests have to order (and pay for) 200 oysters at full price from the restaurant's oyster bar. He provides a tally card for this purpose.

Customers become official members of the oyster club by completing their purchase requirements and paying a $20 initiation fee. A brass plate with their name engraved is added to the oyster club membership plaque and they receive a membership card that entitles them to happy hour prices on oysters, clams, and shrimp at any time. They also receive a golf shirt with the oyster club logo. Mark reports nearly 1,000 diners have become oyster club members in the past 5 years.

Get Your Staff Involved

64

Your Staff *Is* the Restaurant

For most people, the relationship between the staff and the guests *is* your restaurant. It is the quality of the interaction between Betty Lou, the waitress, and the guests at the table that determines what diners think of your place. So while educating the management is important, if that education does not make it to the hourly level, the organization will never realize its full potential.

After conducting literally hundreds of sessions for the hourly staff, I realize that servers are not motivated entirely by tips. Still, it is hard to deny that tip income is the major portion of their income in most restaurants. Accordingly, this section offers a few thoughts for servers with regard to tips and tipping in the real world, taken from my book, *50 Tips to Improve Your Tips: The Service Pro's Pocket Guide to Delighting Diners.*

If you don't get copies of *50 Tips* for everyone, at least share the ideas with them in preshift meetings. Everyone will benefit.

This section also discusses three other very effective practices that your staff can use to make guests want to come back that one extra time a month—showing gratitude, making a personal recommendation, and actually inviting guests to return.

This is not all your staff needs to know to effectively be part of the sales-building process, of course, but the topics in this section are all areas where your crew can act pretty much on their own without the need for management permissions or policy changes.

Your staff is the vehicle for implementing every idea presented in this book. They are the ones who determine whether your guests are delighted or not. They are the ones who educate your guests and give them things to talk about. They provide the personal connection that your guests crave. They are the first to learn of most guest complaints and they execute many of the programs that will result in building repeat patronage, sales, and profitability.

Read on and see what your staff can do to help make your guests happier and more inclined to return.

65

Tips and Tipping

Author's Note: This chapter is excerpted from *50 Tips to Improve Your Tips* and as such is written for the service staff. Rather than rewrite it to shift the focus to a management audience, I have chosen to leave it unchanged as perhaps, a model that will help you convey these ideas to your servers.

You have chosen to make your living, at least for awhile, in the hospitality industry—one of the few places people go these days expecting to have a good time. What a great place to be!

A unique feature of the service business is the practice of tipping. For most professional service folks, tips are effectively their entire source of income. Now you can love tipping or you can hate it, but you can't argue that tips are instant feedback on how your guests feel about your work.

The quality of the interaction with your guests not only establishes your income; it also effectively determines how they feel about your restaurant, so in many ways, the success of the business is also in your hands!

Every service pro wants to do a better job (and make more money) and this little book can help you do just that. It will give you valuable insights into how you can make your guests feel better served and it will help you see how to create a relationship with your guests that can cause them to leave you more at the end of the meal and be more anxious to return.

If you take these ideas to heart and make them part of your service style, you should see the results where it counts—in your pocket!

There are basically two ways to build your tips: you can increase your sales and/or you can improve the percentage you receive from each sale. Let's look at these two options and how they may figure into your financial future.

Option 1: Increase Your Sales

Tip income is a percentage of what your guests purchase, so higher sales are likely to mean greater tips.

The approach most people take to build sales is to increase the check through a technique called "suggestive selling." Done with sincerity and skill, it can be very effective. Done poorly, suggestive selling can come across as insincere, shallow, and manipulative.

Another problem is that if your attention is focused on how much money your guests are spending, it can be a distraction that might get in the way of establishing a personal connection with your guests—and it is the level of personal connection that determines how well served your guests feel.

So your tips really come from serving people, not from serving food. If you get the big sale tonight and lose the guests' future business in the process, then pushing the check average was not a very smart strategy for maximizing your income over the long term.

Another way to achieve sales growth is to have your guests return more often. When you focus on repeat patronage, your goal is to delight your guests rather than simply trying to increase sales (although the two are not necessarily incompatible).

Repeat patronage is the safest way to build sales volume. Take a guest who normally comes in twice a month. If you can treat someone in such a way that he or she comes in just one more time a month instead of going to a competitor, you have just increased your sales from this person by 50%—without any increase in the average check and without any pressure on the diner.

Option 2: Increase Your Tip Percentage

If your guests left a bigger percentage of the check as a tip, you would also increase your income. So, for example, if your tips went from 10% to 20% of sales, then you could double your income on the same sales volume!

Your tip percentage may be determined in a number of ways. Some people tip because it is the custom in this country (and if you have served guests from other countries you know that in many cultures tipping is definitely *not* the custom)! Some people will leave a tip, even if the service was poor, because they would feel guilty if they didn't.

But the biggest factor in tipping—the thing that will determine whether diners leave you 10% or 30%—is the level of personal connection you establish with your guests. The greater the bond, the higher your tip is likely to be. At the least, when the guest is deciding what to leave you at the end of the meal, personal connection will cause them to round up instead of rounding down!

Do you have regulars who always ask for you? Do you typically get a better tip from them? If so, it shows what personal connection can do for your tip income. The good news is that the same thing can happen with virtually every table . . . and more often than not!

The following section offers some ideas that can help this happen for you. Read on!

66

Tips to Improve Your Tips

Creating guest delight is great fun and the best servers make a game out of it. There is no limit to the possibilities when it comes to guest delight, particularly when you allow yourself to act instinctively in the spirit of fun and service. You must stay within the bounds of good taste and remember that your guests probably are not looking for a buddy.

That being said, if you think too much about an action before you take it, it will lack the sincerity and personal interest that is essential to creating personal connection. Actions taken in the moment are always more positive. That does not mean that you cannot consider possibilities in advance and figure out how you might handle them if they seem appropriate.

In other words, do your homework, then clear your mind, connect with your guests, and trust your instincts. To give you a few ideas, here are some suggestions for servers taken from my book, *50 Tips to Improve Your Tips: The Service Pro's Guide to Delighting Diners*. Again, I have left the focus on the service staff.

Acknowledge guests within 60 seconds   Were you ever seated in a restaurant only to wait . . . and wait? Do you recall how that affected your mood? Would it surprise you to learn that there is a relationship between a person's mood and their enjoyment of the meal? Would you expect a better tip from a guest in a good mood or a bad one? Your initial contact sets the tone for the rest of the meal. Guests just feel more comfortable if they know the server is aware that they are waiting. The longer they sit without contact, the more irritated they get. Even if you are busy, come to the table, stop, focus your attention, smile, extend a friendly welcome, and let them know you will be right back. If you are too buried to start their service within 3 minutes, ask for help.

Look at guests when you speak to them   You won't make points by talking to the tablecloth or your order pad. When speaking to guests, clear your head, try to engage their eyes, and smile.

Even if they do not look back at you, they will sense your focus. When addressing a table of guests, shift your attention from one diner to another every few seconds and speak *only* to the person you are looking at. You will hold the attention of the entire table and they will *all* feel better served. Another thing: Never talk to a table while you are moving. When you do, you are effectively saying that you have something more important happening and you don't want to be delayed. The only result is that you look like a jerk and your guests feel less significant.

Keep your mind off the tip   A healthy tip results from taking proper care of your guests and creating a personal connection with them. Interestingly, when you fixate on the reward, it is a distraction that can prevent you from giving your full attention to the activities and attitudes that will actually produce that reward. When you are distracted, your guests are more likely to feel unserved and less inclined to leave a good tip. So if you don't think about your tip during the meal, you are likely to earn more. So what do you think about? Nothing! Keep your head clear and deal only with what is happening at the moment. Time will fly, you will stay out of the weeds, and your guests will have a better time!

Reinforce the guest's decisions   Nobody likes to make a mistake, so people can feel particularly vulnerable whenever they have to make a decision. As an extreme example, imagine how you would feel if you ordered something and the waiter rolled his eyes and laughed! A few encouraging comments from you can reassure your guests that they are making wise choices. The better they feel about their decisions, the more likely they will be to order additional items and try new things. Even if what they choose is not your favorite, you can still reinforce the decision. Try something like "That's one of our most popular (most interesting) items." "Jack, one of our waiters, just raves about that!" "I think you're really going to like that!" You get the idea.

Pass some good news to the cooks   In the same way that you need to be sensitive to the mood of your guests, you will also benefit from being sensitive to the kitchen crew. If you have the support of the kitchen, it will be a lot easier to take exceptionally good care of your guests! Think about it. The cooks are back there knocking themselves out to produce great product under extreme conditions and the only time they hear about it is when something is wrong! To help foster harmony, try to share some good news with the cooks on your trips to the kitchen. Don't break their concentration, but be sure to let them know when guests are loving the food. P.S.: Treat the dish crew with respect, too. They can also help you out!

Recognize lefties   The standard service setting (position of the water glass, coffee cup, etc.) is set up for right-handed people. Most of the time this is not an issue, but it can occasionally present a minor irritation for your left-handed guests. If you are a lefty, you know what I mean. If you are not, watch how a left-handed diner will often move the water glass, etc. to the left side where it is easier to grasp naturally. If you notice that a guest is left-handed, serve the beverages on the left (or wherever they have been placed). There is no right or wrong issue here, strictly a matter of making it as easy as possible for the guest. It's a small touch, but it will show that you notice and that your guest's well-being is important to you.

Move with the speed of the room   Good service is invisible. That is, it never detracts guests from the reason they came out—to be with their companions and enjoy a pleasant meal. A frantic server charging around in an otherwise calm dining room can be a major distraction for guests. When it happens, it may diminish both their experience of the meal and your tip. To avoid this lapse of service, try being invisible by moving "at the speed of the room." This means that if the pace of the meal is lively, move more quickly. If the feeling is relaxed, your movements should be slower. If you move at the speed of the room, your activities will never be a distraction and your guests will have a better time. It takes some practice but it can be fun!

Ask permission before refilling coffee   If you take your coffee any way but black, you know that coffee drinkers have a certain balance of coffee, cream, and sugar that they really like. If you top off the cup without permission, you upset that balance and risk irritating the guest. Just ask permission before you refill the cup and you will stand out from most of your competitors. The same holds true for iced tea or any other beverage that the diner may have "doctored up" to taste. Be sure, too, that guests always know when you have refilled a cup with hot coffee. People can block out anything and you certainly don't want an accidental scalding because a diner didn't notice that you added hot coffee to a cup they expected to be cooler!

Invite guests back on a specific day for a specific reason
The safest way to build sales is by getting guests to return more often. "Y'all come back now" is pleasant, but it isn't very likely to move people to action. You will generate more repeat business with something specific. If it seems appropriate, consider a comment like "Please come back next Thursday for our fajita special. It's really a great deal. I'll be working that night and I would really enjoy seeing you again." This is more likely to generate a return visit than a simple "thank you." Inviting guests to ask for you on their return is a good way to build a regular following. You probably have a few loyal patrons already and today's strangers can be tomorrow's regulars.

REMEMBER: Guests only leave good tips because *they* want to!

50 Tips to Improve Your Tips: The Service Pro's Guide to Delighting Diners, is available in a pocket-sized paperback book. See "Resources" on page 203.

67

Show Gratitude

No matter what else you do, it is essential that you show the depth of your gratitude for your guests' patronage. Nobody gets all the appreciation they deserve. That they chose your restaurant in the first place is significant and all the more so because they are probably trying you out because some other operator dropped the ball with them.

More than any choice of words, **gratitude is conveyed in the feeling behind your tone of voice** when you speak to your guests thank them for their patronage or invite them to return.

To get in touch with that feeling, start by reminding yourself that your guests had a lot of options when deciding where to dine . . . including many places that were less expensive and perhaps more convenient than coming into your restaurant. They are probably dealing with a number of struggles in both their personal and professional life (who isn't?).

You have been given the opportunity to "make their day" and restore their faith in human nature. What an incredible privilege! As if that wasn't enough, they are likely to leave a tip that reflects, as much as anything, the degree of human connection the server has been able to establish with them.

If you will permit yourself to get in touch with these feelings before you open your mouth, your guests will be touched by your gratitude and remember you more favorably. From this feeling, anything you say will work.

At the least, you must thank them for their patronage. This must be done by more people than just the server at the table. The manager should try to thank every guest personally and the greeters should also try to extend a final sincere thank-you to every departing guest (ideally as they hold the door open for them!). If there are parking lot attendants, they should also be brought into the loop.

A note to managers   Your staff will treat your guests the way *you* treat your staff. Your interactions with your crew must reflect the gratitude that you want them to convey to your guests. You are a role model whether you want the job or not!

68

Make a Personal Recommendation

I have risked the wrath of the foodservice gods by questioning the wisdom of the technique of building the check by suggestive selling techniques. My premise is that savvy operators should seek to increase sales by building guest loyalty, not the check average.

Just so there is no misunderstanding, I am not suggesting that you stand there quietly waiting for the guest to order. There is, however, a less risky method to increase sales and that is to make a personal recommendation.

In my staff seminars, I explain to servers the risks of selling techniques and they pick up on it right away. In fact, I once received a standing ovation from a group of servers when I reassured them that I was not going to give them another lecture on suggestive selling!

Instead, I suggested that they forget about trying to sell and simply make a personal recommendation to their guests.

I advise servers, "Tell the guest what *you* like. Tell them what *you* think is the best thing on the menu. Tell them what *you* plan to have when you get off your shift. It is your natural enthusiasm and sincerity that makes this work, and you can only be enthusiastic about what you truly like."

The best part of this approach is that servers do not have to worry about alienating the guests. If a waiter raves about one item and the guests are interested in something else, they will ask about it—no problem. A server will not lose points with a guest for having an opinion or for getting excited about what is on your menu.

Besides, sharing favorites with a guest is a lot more personal . . . and certainly easier than trying to guess what a stranger might want. Experienced servers usually recommend two different favorites in each menu category—appetizers, entrees, desserts, etc.—to improve the odds of hitting on something the guest will identify with, but the key is still enthusiasm and sincerity.

Not every server will like every item on the menu, so it would make for a very productive staff meeting if every server shared what their favorite menu item was and why they felt that way about it. This information will allow each server to tap the enthusiasm of the others in the interest of making guests feel better about the choices they make.

A secondary benefit is that the staff responses might identify menu items that nobody likes. If that happens—and unless the unpopular dishes are runaway favorites with your guests—I suggest you either find a way to make these duds exciting or take them off the menu!

To illustrate the point, let's say that Cindy, a server who does not eat red meat, thinks your stir-fried vegetables are the best thing on the menu. Another waiter, Don, is fanatical about your prime rib sandwich. A scene at Cindy's table could go like this:

> Cindy: I'm so glad you could join us tonight. (Small talk) We've got some interesting items that aren't on our regular menu, let me tell you about them. (Describes specials.)
>
> Guest: They sound good but nothing strikes a particular chord with me. What do *you* think is the best thing on the menu?
>
> Cindy: Well, my personal favorite is the veggie stir-fry. The chef cooks it in this great sesame-garlic sauce, the vegetables are nice and fresh and because they are cooked so quickly, they stay nice and crunchy. It's low in fat, very healthy, and you really get a lot for the money!
>
> Guest: I have a meeting this afternoon and I'm not too sure about the garlic. What do you think about the prime rib sandwich?
>
> Cindy: Let me tell you, Don—he's one of our waiters who's been here almost since we opened—well, Don is nuts about the prime rib sandwich. I swear that man would *live* on prime rib if he could! Besides, I've never served it to a guest who didn't rave about it!
>
> Guest: OK, let me try the prime rib sandwich. I'll see if Don knows what he's talking about!

You can see how smooth and easy that can be. The entire exchange is cordial and there is no sales pressure.

Cindy can use Don's enthusiasm to reinforce the guest's decision without the need to mention that she is a vegetarian—information the guest does not care about anyway. She establishes a personal relationship with the guest, helps him make a good decision and the diner feels comfortable about what he ordered.

Does it work? I presented this idea at an in-house service staff seminar one morning. When I came back after lunch that day to do a follow-up session with the managers, a server sought me out. Her eyes were wide and she was excited. She said "*Every* table at my station ordered appetizers at lunch today! It was so much fun—I didn't have to do *anything*!" All she did was tell the guests what *she* liked and they said "It sounds good. We'll try it!"

A Wolf in Sheep's Clothing?

Now I suppose you could argue that making recommendations is just suggestive selling by another name. While the results can be similar, there are several significant differences:

- Making recommendations is a very natural process that your staff will not resist. They do not think of it as selling because they are expressing their *own* ideas, not someone else's. I also find that most servers really enjoy turning their guests on to something particularly good or unusual.

- This approach is not offensive to guests. It is a personal exchange and there is never any implied pressure to buy. Guests will naturally look to the server for inside information on the menu and nobody really believes that "everything is good here!" Even if that is true, it is not particularly helpful as a recommendation.

- You acknowledge your servers as responsible adults with the intelligence to judge what is appropriate to make the guest's experience enjoyable. It may be making a recommendation . . . and it may be saying nothing at all. The server is the only one who can gauge it.

- Because the process is natural and chatty, it helps create a more personal connection between the staff and the guests. This personal connection can help the guest identify more closely with the restaurant and leads to a higher tip percentage for the server.

- Your service staff will *love* you. They will be thrilled that you finally got off it about suggestive selling! After all, most of them have fought you on the idea all along!

What Does It Take?

Obviously, for the servers to make meaningful recommendations, they must have a few favorite items. This requires that they have tasted *everything* you offer. (I remember once asking a waitress what she thought about a lobster casserole listed on the menu. Her reply was, "I don't know, they won't let us order it!" Am I the only one who finds this brilliant cost-saving policy to be incredibly short-sighted?)

Ideally the service staff should watch how each item is prepared so they can talk to the guests from personal experience rather than from memory. Your servers must express themselves in the words that are most natural to them. Scripted communications will just put everyone, guests and servers alike, back into the manipulative world of sales techniques.

To carry this idea a little farther, do you want the staff to recommend a wine to go with each entree? To make this a personal recommendation, they must have tasted your wines in combination with each menu item and come up with a personal favorite.

Often a wine will taste quite different with food than it will by itself. Since you typically sell the two together, it makes sense to taste them together. Discovering the nuances of wine and food and sharing these findings with guests can really be fun for everyone.

By all means, servers should have an opinion on appetizers, desserts, after-dinner drinks, and all those other items that usually make it onto the suggestive selling list. We need to give diners the opportunity to indulge themselves (if they want to) and to sample those items that set us apart from our competitors.

But to be effective, your staff must be sharing *their* excitement, not the management's.

The important point for managers is not to try and force this behavior on your service staff. Your crew will find their own unique way to share their opinions with the guests, and scripting can be dangerous.

If someone on your crew gets stuck for an idea, however, a phrase that always worked well for me started, "Have you ever tried . . . ?"

No matter how the guest answers the question, you have the start of a discussion without any fear of being confrontational.

Remember that the intent is to increase repeat business, not (necessarily) to increase the guest check. Your initial goal is simply to treat guests in a way that will make them want to return.

In most operations, if you can get guests back just one additional time a month, it will give you a 15–50% volume increase . . . and making personal recommendations is an important way that your staff can help.

69

Invite Guests to Return

Have you ever been out to eat and been ignored once you paid the check? When you think about the place where that happened, do you feel anxious to return?

You know the cliché that you don't get a second chance for a first impression. It is also true that the quality of your *last* impression may well determine if you get a second chance at all.

The last impression diners have of your restaurant may well be the one they remember. If it is a positive memory, they will be more inclined to think of you favorably and more likely to return. Since our goal in building sales without selling is simply to treat our guests in such a way that they return just one additional time each month, it is important to make sure that the final impression is positive.

Get Specific

To really affect repeat patronage, it is not enough just to invite people back. "Y'all come back now," is friendly enough, but it is unlikely to move people to action.

To increase dining frequency, I suggest that you *invite guests back on a specific day for a specific reason!* Try some of these lines and see how they feel to you:

> "Come back next Tuesday. We've got an all-you-can eat fish fry."

> "If you liked that blackened sea bass, be sure to come back next Thursday. The chef is planning a special Cajun shrimp etouffé. We sampled a little this afternoon and it was incredible! It will probably go fast, so if you plan to come in, give me a call and I'll be sure to save you some!"

To do this, everyone on the service staff must know what specials are planned for the next week and tastings must be conducted far enough in advance that the staff will be able to make their recommendations from personal experience. This includes greeters and bar staff as well.

Remember that enthusiasm and sincerity are the difference between a warm, personal recommendation and a cold, impersonal sales pitch.

Get Personal

I suspect that people identify more with people more than they identify with organizations.

To maximize the degree of personal connection that guests feel toward the restaurant, I make the following suggestions to servers: *Invite guests back on a day when you will be working and invite them to ask for your station.*

Since they will not be strangers to you on their return visit, you will be more likely to remember their names and to recall what they like or don't like. (You might want to make some notes to be sure.) You are also more likely to get a higher tip percentage from your regulars.

Look over the following example and see what a nice dimension the invitation adds to the final conversation and to the memories that guests take away with them:

> "Have you ever been to our Wednesday night spaghetti feed? It's a little crazier than usual around here but you get a lot of food for a very reasonable price and I know you'll have a great time! It's becoming so popular that reservations might be a good idea. I would take it as a personal compliment if you asked to be seated at my station when you call in. Wednesday is one of my favorite nights around here and I would really enjoy serving you again. I'll even make sure to save you a piece of the chocolate suicide cake!"

Building sales without selling is a simple process with a simple goal—to treat guests in a way that will make them return just one additional time a month.

Your mission now is clear:

First, you must be personally and passionately committed to the idea. People will do what they see you doing, not what they hear you saying. Your personal actions will reinforce the notion of guest delight more surely than any management pep talk.

If this idea only gets lip service from management, it is merely manipulation and all it will get you is a crew who leaves your guests feeling manipulated.

Second, you must structure your training to consistently reinforce the four steps in the program: making a personal recommendation, focusing on guest delight, giving people something to talk about, and inviting guests back on a specific day for a specific reason. Role-playing, coaching, rewards, and positive reinforcement are all necessary pieces of your sales-building program.

Finally, you must monitor your results and make corrections to the system as necessary to be sure that you consistently execute your plan. Remember that when something goes wrong, the breakdown is in your system, not in your staff.

The best part of this idea is that everybody wins.

- The guest has a memorable, hassle-free experience that makes them want to return more often and tell their friends about you.
- Your staff has less pressure, provides more personal service, and makes better tips.
- Management looks at increasing sales and profits from an operation that seems to almost run itself!

These are truly worthy (and entirely realistic) goals. Good luck!

70

Get the Message to Your Staff

Now what? You (hopefully) have a headful of new ideas and are eager to call a staff meeting and get started. But when was the last time you held a really world-class staff meeting? I'm talking about a gathering that was so enjoyable and productive that people left more energized than when they arrived! Did you even realize that such a meeting was possible?

If the idea of a truly invigorating staff meeting seems foreign to your experience, you are not alone. The sad fact is that most staff meetings . . . aren't! In practice, those gatherings we call staff meetings are typically little more than management sermons. Worse yet, they are often presented in a distracted, condescending manner that causes the crew to roll back their eyes, shut down their brains, and experience a serious drop in energy. No wonder everybody dreads them.

A truly effective staff meeting is more about reaching a meeting of the minds than simply accomplishing a gathering of the bodies, and our old models just don't work. If you are willing to take a different approach to staff meetings, they can help you head off emergencies before they arise, reduce the number of problems that require your attention, lower your turnover, and generally help create a smoother-running, more profitable operation.

For the purposes of this text, I am talking about pre-shift meetings as distinguished from more formal sessions devoted exclusively to skill training. The process I am outlining here will generally apply to training sessions, although there will necessarily be more time for the meeting itself and more time devoted to the content of the meeting. At any rate, forget everything you ever knew about staff meetings and let's take a fresh look.

Goals

The primary purpose of staff meetings should be to create a positive feeling in the group. This may sound strange until you realize that a positive feeling helps people naturally recognize what they have in common. When the feeling in the group is warm and supportive, it is easier to see that everyone is in it together and the success of the group is inseparable from the success of each individual. Without a good feeling, people tend to stay focused on their differences.

This close feeling is more likely to result from an appreciative sharing of the good news—and there is usually quite a bit when you look for it. Staff meetings are not the time to address individual shortcomings—that should be done one-on-one in private—and they are certainly not an appropriate time to dwell on group failings.

From a supportive feeling, staff meetings will naturally lead to the second goal—opening a dialogue. A dialogue is a comfortable two-way flow of ideas that leaves all the participants feeling connected and important. The staff can learn from you and you can learn from them. With this sort of rapport, your meetings naturally tend to instill understanding rather than simply passing along knowledge. The difference is significant because understanding "sticks" where information is soon forgotten.

Additionally, the flow of ideas back to management helps eliminate the "them and us" mentality and helps your staff feel that it is also *their* restaurant. By bringing your staff into the loop—by soliciting, considering, and valuing their ideas—staff meetings can help establish and enhance the feeling of teamwork in the operation. This is likely to result in improved guest service, productivity, and profitability.

The third objective of effective staff meetings is training. Properly conducted staff meetings are a forum for continuous improvement. Even if you have a structured training program, good operators never miss a chance to pass along a few more hints, and this is a perfect opportunity to do it. If you don't train, you deliver one of two messages: either that you are getting exactly the results you want and you can't possibly get any better or that any ninny can instinctively be successful in the foodservice business without training. I doubt that either case is true.

As Hap Gray, owner of the Watermark Restaurant in Cleveland so wisely told me, "My training program is the only thing that makes this *my* restaurant. If I didn't train, I'd only be a caretaker for the bank and not an owner!"

Considerations

When you decide to get serious about staff meetings, it is critical that you commit to holding them on a regular basis—ideally before every shift every day—no matter what is going on that day. When meetings are held sporadically or are frequently canceled because of other pressures (and there are *always* other pressures), it tells your staff the true importance you give these meetings. If staff meetings are not important to you, they will certainly not be important to your crew.

Ideally, pre-shift meetings should last 10 or 15 minutes. Any shorter and you don't have enough time to get anything done; any longer and you may start to lose people's attention. Pick a specific meeting length and stick with it. Make a commitment to start and end precisely on time.

Bear in mind that while your service staff may be getting paid during the meeting, they are not receiving tips and it is disrespectful to take advantage of their time. Remember, too, that pre-shift meetings are just as essential for the kitchen staff as for the servers. Daily tasting of specials and new menu items are also important, but it is the type of activity that can easily be handled between the kitchen and service staffs outside of the pre-shift meeting and without the direction of management.

Mindset

The factor that most determines whether or not a staff meeting will be effective is the thinking of the manager or supervisor conducting it.

Think about it. Do you approach your job like a cop, finding and correcting mistakes, or do you define your job as a coach, identifying and building on inherent strengths? Do you see your staff as bunch of goof-offs looking for a free ride or as a group of intelligent adults who want to do the best job they can? Do you think that management has to have all the answers or do you view your role as helping your crew discover the answers for themselves?

What you see is what you get. Recognize that true learning comes from the inside out rather than from the outside in. When you have your own head in the right place, you can finally start to conduct staff meetings that will build confidence and involvement in your staff.

Now that you understand that it is possible to hold energizing staff meetings, you may be anxious to get started. To help you get things rolling, here is a suggested format for a 10–15 minute pre-shift meeting:

Good news (1–2 minutes)   The purpose here is to recognize what is working and set a positive tone for the meeting. You can talk about progress made toward a particular goal, share a success story about one of the staff, or read a complimentary letter from a guest. Everybody likes to hear good news and it will help establish a warm feeling for the rest of the session, particularly when delivered with a feeling of sincere gratitude.

News of the day (2–3 minutes)   In this segment you might talk briefly about what is coming up on this shift and in the near future. You could mention special parties or promotions in effect. You could use it to outline your not-on-the-menu items (specials) for the day. The important thing is that you be very focused and very brief. Don't get lost in this part of the program or you run the risk of sermonizing and that can kill the mood.

Staff comments (5 minutes)   This is when you open the floor to the crew. It is the most important part of the meeting because it is when you can really find out what is happening and what is on people's minds. The critical skill is to listen without judging the comments you receive. Let yourself be really stupid for awhile. Listen with curiosity. Try to avoid preconceived notions about what people might be saying and be cautious about injecting your own thoughts into the discussion.

This may take some practice, but the results will be worth the effort. Your goal is to create a safe environment for people to share their ideas and to learn from each other. This is where that all-important dialogue we discussed earlier really begins.

At first, you may find that people are reluctant to open up. You will soon discover that the quality and quantity of the input you receive will be in direct proportion to how well your staff feels you are listening to what they say—not just *hearing* the words but really listening to understand the message. Your willingness to consider their ideas will build trust and you will get more and more involvement from your crew as the level of trust in the organization improves.

If your initial efforts to get people talking are greeted with silence, here are a few questions that may prompt some discussion: Who deserves to be thanked or recognized and for what? What is making your job tough? What have you noticed that is improving? What are we doing that we shouldn't be doing? What *aren't* we doing that we *should* be doing? Where is the system breaking down? What questions came up on your last shift that you couldn't answer? If this were your restaurant, what would you change about it? You get the idea.

As people are talking, give them your undistracted attention and really *listen* for the feeling behind their words. You may want to ask if other people see things the same way as the speaker. You may want to ask a clarifying question to be sure you understand but resist the urge to add too many of your own comments. The purpose of this part of the meeting is to get information flowing in your direction so that you can learn from your crew and start to see the operation from their point of view.

In my experience, if you will only ask for comments (and be passionately interested in the answers), your staff will tell you everything you need to know about what it will take to make the operation more efficient. When you have a consensus, seriously consider what you have learned. See if you can take some action based on their ideas because when people see something actually happening because of their input, they will gain hope and tell you even more.

This is not management by committee—the final responsibility for action always rests with management. It is, however, an honest acknowledgment that collectively we can usually make better decisions than one person acting alone.

New information/training (3–5 minutes)   Every gathering is an opportunity to enhance skills. Particularly in the beginning, I suggest you shorten the time allocated to training by the time that the staff comments segment runs long. It is probably more important that you learn from the crew than that they learn from you.

Once they have confidence that there is a forum where their ideas will be heard and considered, your staff will be ready to receive new information. Use this part of the meeting to discuss a single point you want the staff to focus on for that shift, to impart some product knowledge, to share professional tips, or to reinforce or supplement material from your regular training program.

Again, your own focus is important. Cut to the chase and don't ramble. People will be watching the time and you will build credibility by being direct and finishing on time.

Effective staff meetings *are* possible. As your skills and credibility improve, you will see that staff meetings can be an easy way to begin creating a feeling of teamwork in your organization. The exciting part is that they will also let you tap the inherent talents of your staff which will, in turn, help the manager's role evolve into one that is more enjoyable and less stressful.

I realize that this little dissertation may raise as many questions as it answers, so if you have questions, please give me a call and I'll try to fill in any missing pieces. I wish you good luck—let me know how it goes.

Closing
Comments

... But Wait, There's So Much More!

This book only scratches the surface of what is possible. There is so much more that I want to tell you but there is just not the space.

I never got into the stories about Mike Hurst bringing the elephant into his bar at 15th Street Fisheries or about his pajama parties in the parking lot or about how he feeds the pelicans on the dock outside his restaurant every afternoon to draw a crowd.

I didn't mention the Safe House in Milwaukee, a word-of-mouth legend if ever one existed! If I tried to describe it, you wouldn't believe it, so just make it a point to stop there if you are ever in the area.

Other than describing their men's room, I did not talk much about the Madonna Inn in San Luis Obispo, California, another place that must be seen to be believed. Even then you will probably have trouble . . . but I guarantee that you will talk about it!

There was no space to include all the delightful touches found in so many independent restaurants all over the United States and Canada (and the world for that matter), gestures that were the result of someone who cared doing something nice for their guests.

By the time this book is published, I will have visited hundreds of restaurants for the first time and picked up hundreds of new ideas that should have been included in these pages. That is the exciting part of what I do . . . and it can be just as exciting for you.

The Well Never Runs Dry

If you are open to possibilities, you never run out of new ideas. You can see creative ideas in other restaurants, of course, but keep an eye open in retail shops, malls, and virtually everywhere you go.

Look for something you haven't thought of yet and see what it causes you to think of. Even the ideas that at first seem puzzling or stupid may have a grain of brilliance in them that you can adapt for your own benefit. Don't copy someone else's ideas—it is unprofessional and they will never fit— but see what you can adapt to fit your own peculiar situation.

This happens almost automatically when you can show up for your life with a clear mind. The "dumber" you are, the less blinded you are by your preconceived ideas of the way you think things "should be" and the more open you become to fresh possibilities that are outside your present experience. The more possibilities you entertain, the more insights you have and the smarter you get. Funny how that works, isn't it?

My hope is that this book has opened up a few possibilities for you and made you aware of another way of looking at what makes restaurants (or any business for that matter) grow, excel, and prosper. If you grasp the principles behind the notions we have discussed in the preceding pages, you will start to see your own answers. When that happens, there will be no stopping you. Go for it.

Resources

There is always more to learn. For those readers who want to follow up on any of the notions I have discussed in this book, here are a few places to find additional information. The list is not exhaustive—there are many more resources than I am aware of—but this list should give you a place to begin looking.

For your convenience, I have provided phone numbers when available. These numbers are current as of this writing but area codes and phone numbers often change. You may need to go through directory assistance for those numbers that are out of service.

Books

Clarke, Susan, *Secrets of Service: The Story of Making Your Customers Feel Good About Spending Their Money,* 1991, Amerasian Press, (888) WE-MOTIVATE.

Feltenstein, Tom, *Tom Feltenstein's Encyclopedia of Promotional Tactics,* Neighborhood Marketing Institute, 44 Cocoanut Row, Suite T-5, Palm Beach, FL 36830, (561) 655-7822.

Feltenstein, Tom, *Underdog Marketing: Strategies for Taking on the Big Guns,* Neighborhood Marketing Institute, 44 Cocoanut Row, Suite T-5, Palm Beach, FL 36830, (561) 655-7822.

Feltenstein, Tom, *Foodservice Marketing for the '90s: How to Become the #1 Restaurant in Your Neighborhood,* 1992, John Wiley & Sons, Inc., 605 Third Avenue, New York, NY 10158.

LeBoeuf, Michael, *How to Win Customers and Keep Them for Life,* 1987, Berkley Books, 200 Madison Avenue, New York, NY 10016.

Marvin, Bill, *Restaurant Basics: Why Guests Don't Come Back and What You Can Do About It,* 1992, John Wiley & Sons, Inc., 605 Third Avenue, New York, NY 10158.

Marvin, Bill, *The Foolproof Foodservice Selection System: The Complete Manual for Creating a Quality Staff,* 1993, John Wiley & Sons, Inc., 605 Third Avenue, New York, NY 10158.

Marvin, Bill, *From Turnover to Teamwork: How to Build and Retain a Customer-Oriented Foodservice Staff,* 1994, John Wiley & Sons, Inc., 605 Third Avenue, New York, NY 10158.

Marvin, Bill, *50 Tips to Improve Your Tips: The Service Pro's Guide to Delighting Diners,* 1995, Prototype Restaurants, PO Box 280, Gig Harbor, WA 98335, (800) 767-1055.

Marvin Bill, *Cashing in on Complaints: Turning Disappointed Diners Into Gold,* 1997, Hospitality Masters Press, PO Box 280, Gig Harbor, WA 98335, (800) 767-1055.

Marvin, Bill and others, *50 Proven Ways to Build Restaurant Sales & Profit,* 1997, Hospitality Masters Press, PO Box 280, Gig Harbor, WA 98335, (800) 767-1055.

Ries, Al and Trout, Jack, *The 22 Immutable Laws of Marketing,* 1993, HarperCollins Publishers, 10 East 53rd Street, New York, NY 10022.

Ries, Al and Trout, Jack, *Bottom Up Marketing,* 1989, McGraw-Hill, 1221 Avenue of the Americas, New York, NY 10020.

Audio Tapes (call for current catalogs)

Marvin, Bill, Prototype Restaurants, PO Box 280, Gig Harbor, WA 98335 (800) 767-1055.

Slutzky, Jeff, Streetfighter Marketing, 467 Waterbury Ct., Gahanna, OH 43230, (800) 837-7355.

Video Tapes (call for current catalogs)

Feltenstein, Tom, Neighborhood Marketing Institute, 44 Cocoanut Row, Suite T-5, Palm Beach, FL 36830 (561) 655-7822.

Marvin, Bill, Prototype Restaurants, PO Box 280, Gig Harbor, WA 98335 (800) 767-1055.

Newsletters

"Home Remedies," Prototype Restaurants, PO Box 280, Gig Harbor, WA 98335 (bimonthly, subscription), (800) 767-1055.

"Restaurant Marketing Newsletter," Savannah Consulting, 2601 Hibernia Street, Suite C, Dallas, TX 75204, (monthly, subscription), Fax: (214) 754-8067.

"Pro-Motion Marketing Newsletter," National Restaurant Association, 1200–17th Street NW, Washington, DC 20036, (monthly, subscription), (800) 424-4156.

Frequent Diner Software

Customer Knowlogy, 38345–30th Street East, Suite E-4, Palmdale, CA 93550 (805) 267-7722.

Frequent Diner Program Administration

The Customer Connection, 621 South Andreasen Drive, Escondido, CA 92029, (800) 477-7166.

Frequency Systems, 5589 Old Fort Jupiter Road, Jupiter, FL 33458, (407)575-7261.

Guestbook

Plainfield Software, 852 SE 21st Street, Portland, OR 97205, (800) 327-0693.

Cigar Dinner Planning Guide

Cigar Aficionado magazine, 387 Park Avenue South, New York, NY 10016, (212) 684-4224.

Plastic Cards

Credit Card Systems, 180 Shepard Avenue, Wheeling, IL 60090, (800) 747-1269.

Legend Business Systems, 1018 Industry Drive, Seattle, WA 98188, (206) 575-0890.

Echo Plastics, PO Box 69-4217, Miami, FL 33269, (800) 327-0693.

Smoker/Non-Smoker Co-Existence

The Accommodation Program, (800) 800-5197.

About the Author

William R. Marvin

The Restaurant Doctor™

Bill Marvin, "The Restaurant Doctor™," is an advisor to service-oriented businesses across North America. Bill is the founder of Prototype Restaurants, a hospitality consulting and management group, and president of Effortless, Inc., a management research and education company based in the Pacific Northwest.

A veteran of the hospitality industry, his hands-on operational background includes hotels, clubs, restaurants, and institutions. He has had his name on the loans, the keys in his hand, and the payroll to meet. This wide range of experience has contributed to his broad perspective on the service industry and enables him to relate to all types and sizes of service-focused operations.

Bill is a member of the Council of Hotel and Restaurant Trainers and the National Speakers Association. He has been designated a Certified Food Executive by the International Foodservice Executives Association and is one of the first to earn certification as a Foodservice Management Professional from the National Restaurant Association.

He taught a course in food facilities design at Wayne State University in Detroit and conducted a continuing foodservice class for the City of Colorado Springs, Colorado for several years. He is a past Director of the Colorado Restaurant Association for seven years.

He started in the industry at the age of 14, washing dishes (by hand!) in a small restaurant on Cape Cod. He went on to earn a degree in Hotel Administration from Cornell University. Bill moved to Colorado in 1984 to design the foodservice system for the U.S. Olympic Training Centers. He and his wife, Margene, relocated to Gig Harbor, in the Puget Sound area of Washington State, in 1993.

Before joining the Olympic Committee, Bill spent twelve years in San Francisco. He was a supervisor in the management consulting department of an international hospitality consulting firm. He developed and operated two restaurants of his own. He was an independent restaurant consultant specializing in marketing, new concept development, and Chapter 11 reorganizations.

In typical Northern California fashion, he also became a commercial hot air balloon pilot and in the fall of 1981 became the first person to fly hot air balloons in China!

He ran a condominium hotel in the Caribbean, managed a prestigious New England country club, and worked as a consultant/designer for a national food facilities engineering firm. As an officer in the U.S. Navy, he also operated several enlisted feeding facilities, the largest serving over 20,000 meals a day.

Bill has been a featured guest on Hospitality Television and is a regular contributor to national trade magazines in several industries. In addition to his private consulting practice, he is a sought-after speaker for corporate keynote addresses and training seminars across North America.

Internet surfers can get Bill's latest thoughts at http://www.restaurantdoctor.com. For information on his "Home Remedies" newsletter or to contact Bill directly:

EFFORTLESS, INC.
PO Box 280
Gig Harbor, WA 98335
(800) 767-1055
Fax: (888) 851-6887
e-mail: bill@restaurantdoctor.com

Index